CAN'T YOU BASTARDS READ?

BY MARK LYNCH

EVERYTHING YOU NEVER WANTED TO KNOW ABOUT NUCLEAR WARFARE

GRAFTON BOOKS

A Division of the Collins Publishing Group

LONDON GLASGOW
TORONTO SYDNEY AUCKLAND

Grafton Books
A Division of the Collins Publishing Group
8 Grafton Street, London W1X 3LA

A Grafton UK Paperback Original 1988

Reprinted 1988

Copyright © Mark Lynch 1986

ISBN 0-586-20171-8

Printed and bound in Great Britain by
Scotprint Ltd., Musselburgh

Set in Helvetica

All rights reserved. No part of this publication may
be reproduced, stored in a retrieval system, or
transmitted, in any form, or by any means, electronic,
mechanical, photocopying, recording or otherwise,
without the prior permission of the publishers.

This book is sold subject to the condition that it
shall not, by way of trade or otherwise, be lent,
re-sold, hired out or otherwise circulated
without the publisher's prior consent in any
form of binding or cover other than that in
which it is published and without a similar
condition including this condition being imposed
on the subsequent purchaser.

Dedicated to Robert Oppenheimer, for
without him this book would be 80
empty pages and therefore very
difficult to sell!

FOREWORD
by Adrian Edmondson, a Bastard

Dear public,

Yes, I bloody well can read! And may I say that I have never read a book as full of anti-nuclear cartoons as this one! They have obviously been drawn by some crazed pinko neo-Bennite quasi-communist quasi-feminist quasi-modoist black lesbian-type jewish rastafarian whale-saving anti-sexist anti-capitalist anti-mabelist vegetarian homosexual trades unionist bastard, who probably thinks it's funny to fold up a five pound note in such a way as to make it look like the queen is giving someone a blow job.

There are many types of bastard in this world: miserable, stupid, dribbly, farty, Mrs Thatcher, etc., etc.. I myself am an all-round bastard, although after 11 o'clock in the morning I usually specialize in attempting to retain my crown as 'King of the Drinky Bastards' which is why I somfhin lendy ahgtewuy lkhjawqopi sdflk lksdhjepoiw hfcye wpxmms dkjoe jcbsjho and my typing goes all funny, but the crazy paving feminine sexy black vegetable bastard is definitely the worst.

It just won't do, all this 'Oooh, let's save the planet', 'Oooh, look out the world's in danger' innuendo nonsense . . . bring back hanging, I say. Apparently he's an aborigine, so at least he's got no land rights. I mean, all right, let's be rational about this, let's weigh up the pros and cons of nuclear weapons:

PROS	CONS
They look like huge penii	They could blow the whole world apart in 4 minutes

Well, I know which side I'm on! Because what's inside my trousers is often mistaken for a nuclear weapon, actually! And I know I'm going to get all sorts of letters from angry feminine sexys now saying, 'Your problem is that your brain is ruled by your dick, and the same goes for all the world leaders including Mrs Thatcher; most of the aggression in the world can be blamed fairly and squarely on men trying to compensate for the size of their dicks.' Well, I'd like all you fluffy young lesbians to know that I have no need for a dick compensator (and nor does Mrs Thatcher), and if you'd care to send me an s.a.e., I will forward to you a copy of a certificate from my doctor, verifying that my penis is nearly 2″ (2″!) long and including the unsolicited comment 'It's a big one'. I will not enter into any further correspondence on this matter; however, if any of you fancy an on-site inspection, I'm sure something could be arranged.

Finally, I would like to say that I have never met Mark Lynch and that I am writing this foreword purely through financial inducement. I think the book stinks, but please buy it in bulk so that my infinitesimally small percentage may amount to something one day.

Yours with my finger on your button,

ADRIAN EDMONDSON

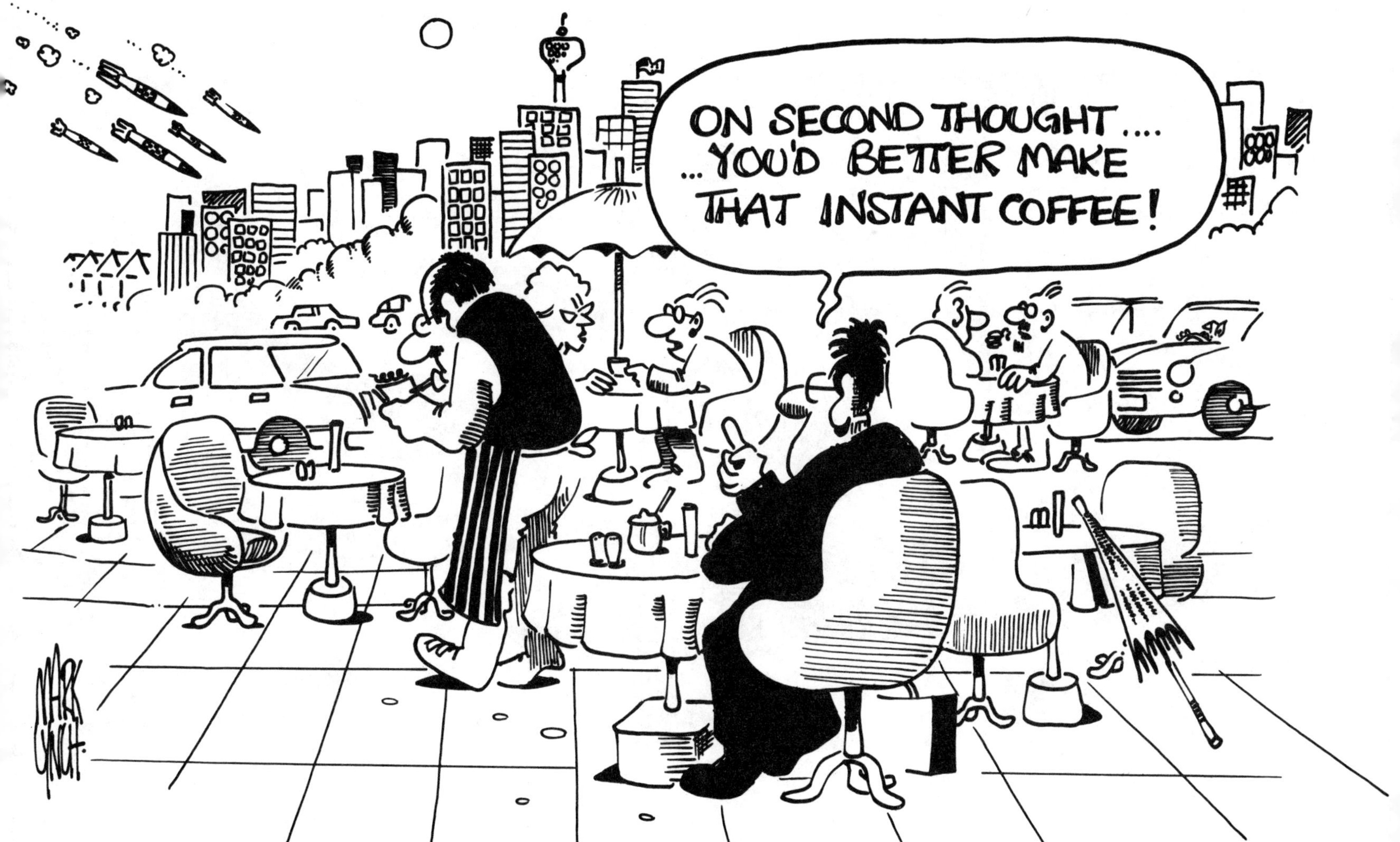
ON SECOND THOUGHT.... ...YOU'D BETTER MAKE THAT INSTANT COFFEE!
MARK LYNCH

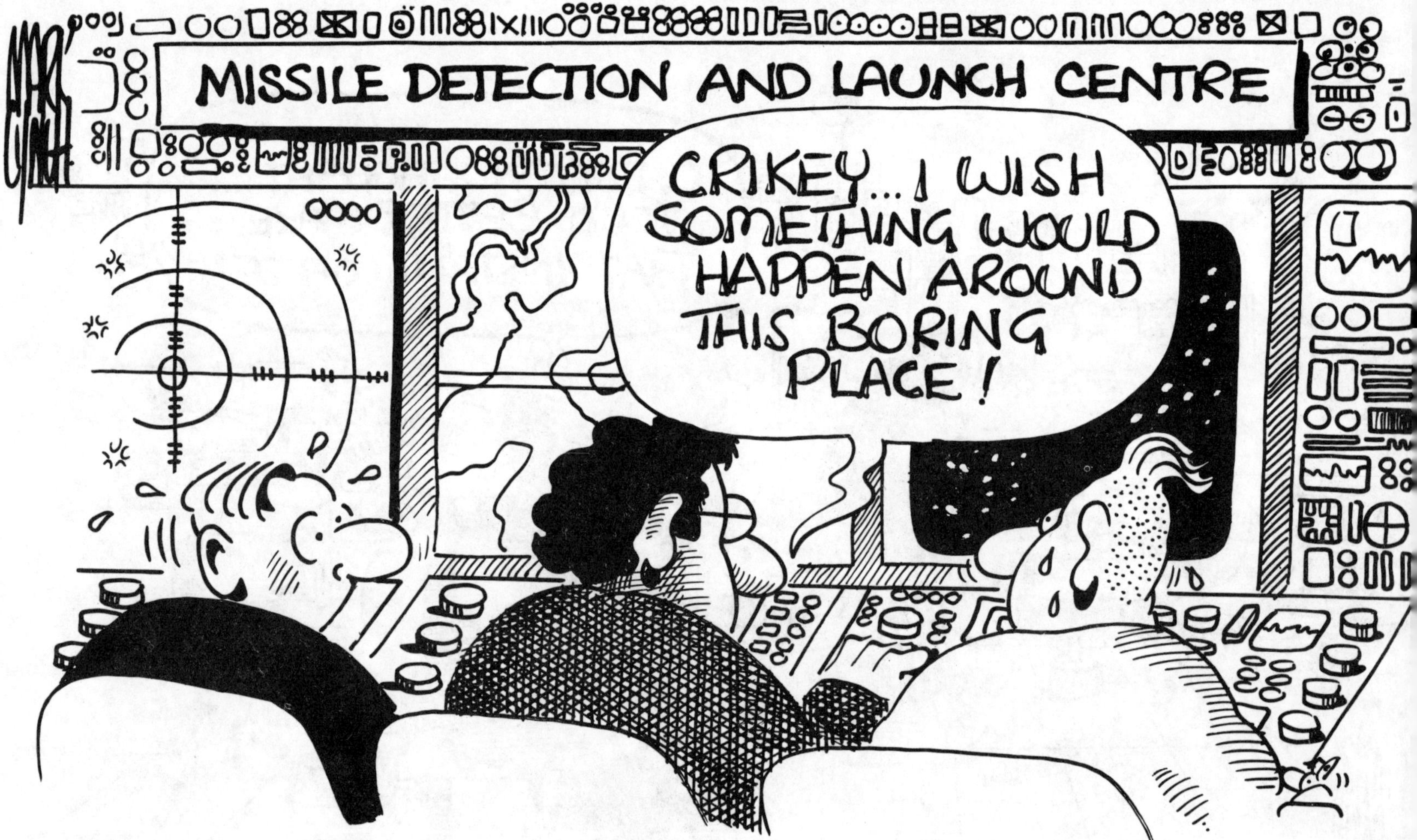
MISSILE DETECTION AND LAUNCH CENTRE
CRIKEY... I WISH SOMETHING WOULD HAPPEN AROUND THIS BORING PLACE!

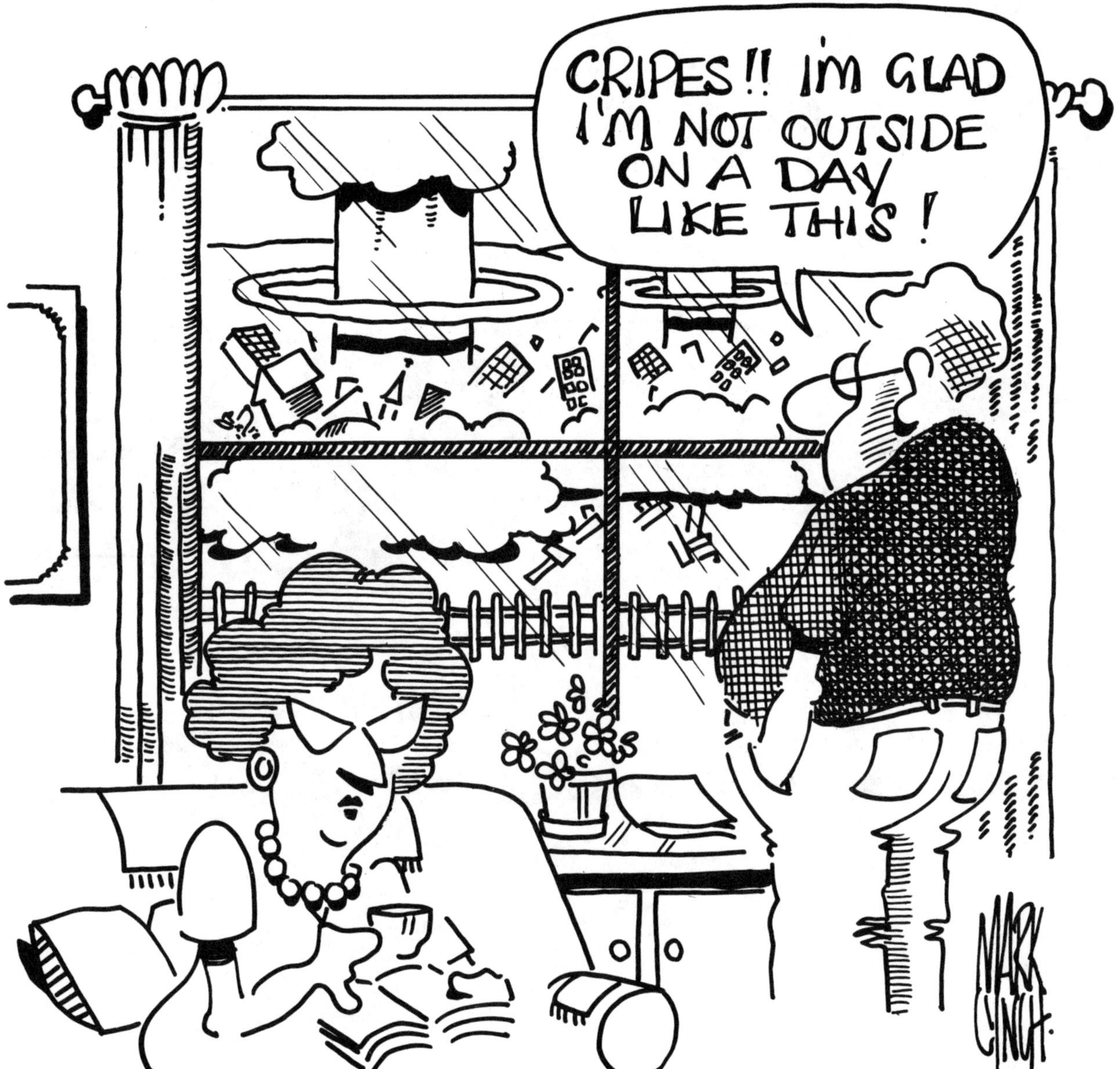
CRIPES!! I'M GLAD I'M NOT OUTSIDE ON A DAY LIKE THIS!
MARK LYNCH.

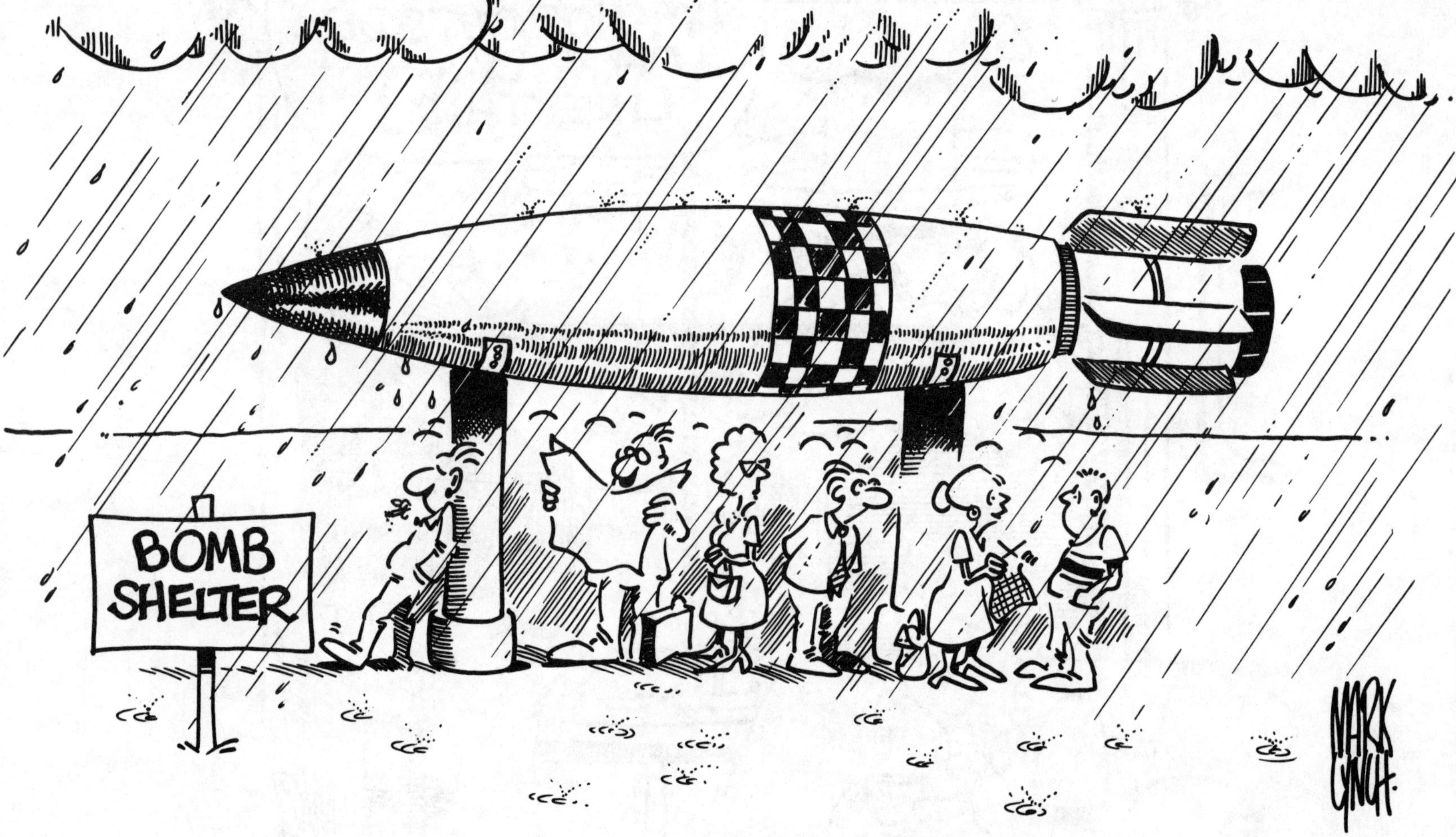
BOMB
SHELTER
MARK
LYNCH.

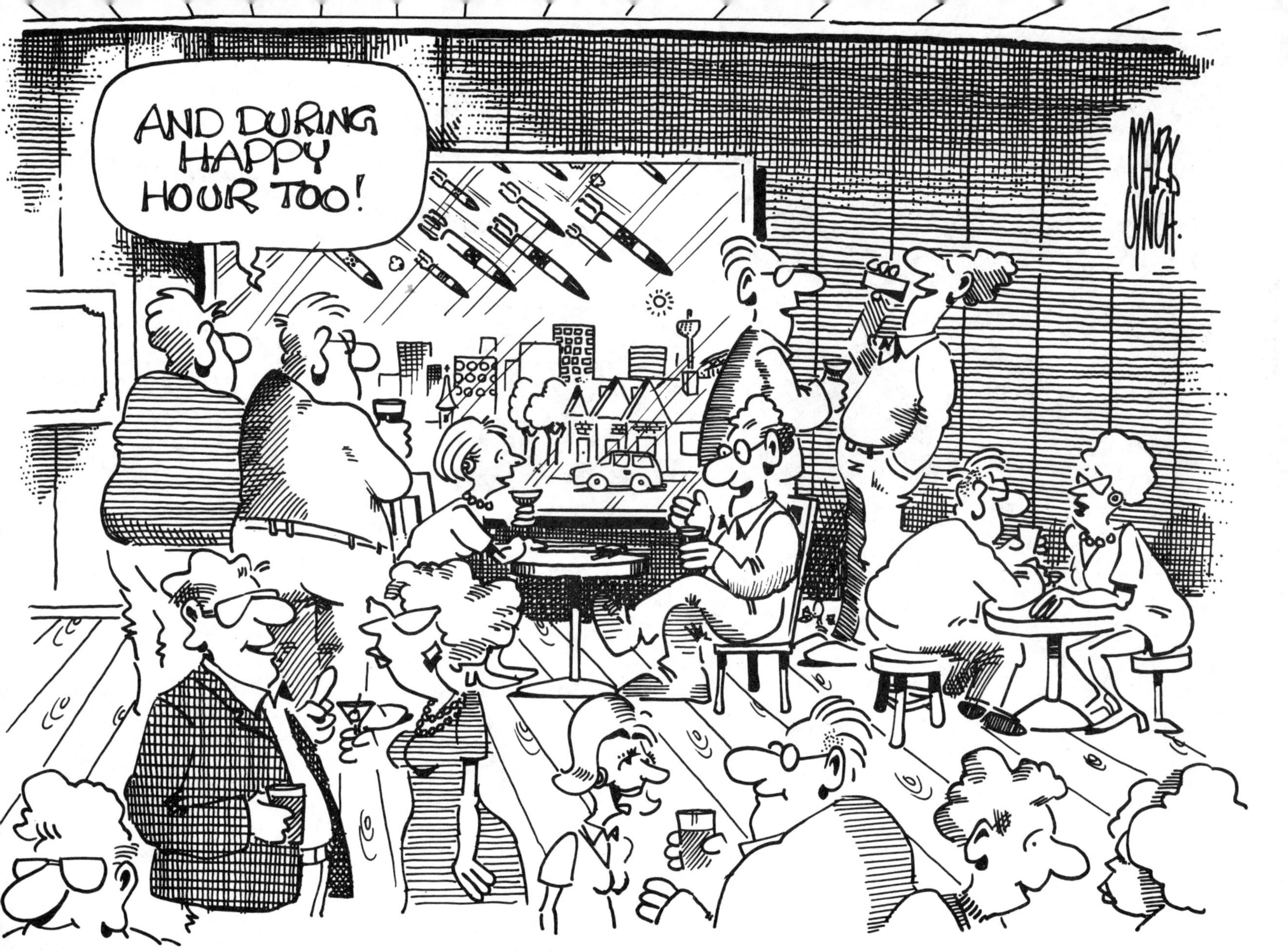
AND DURING HAPPY HOUR TOO!

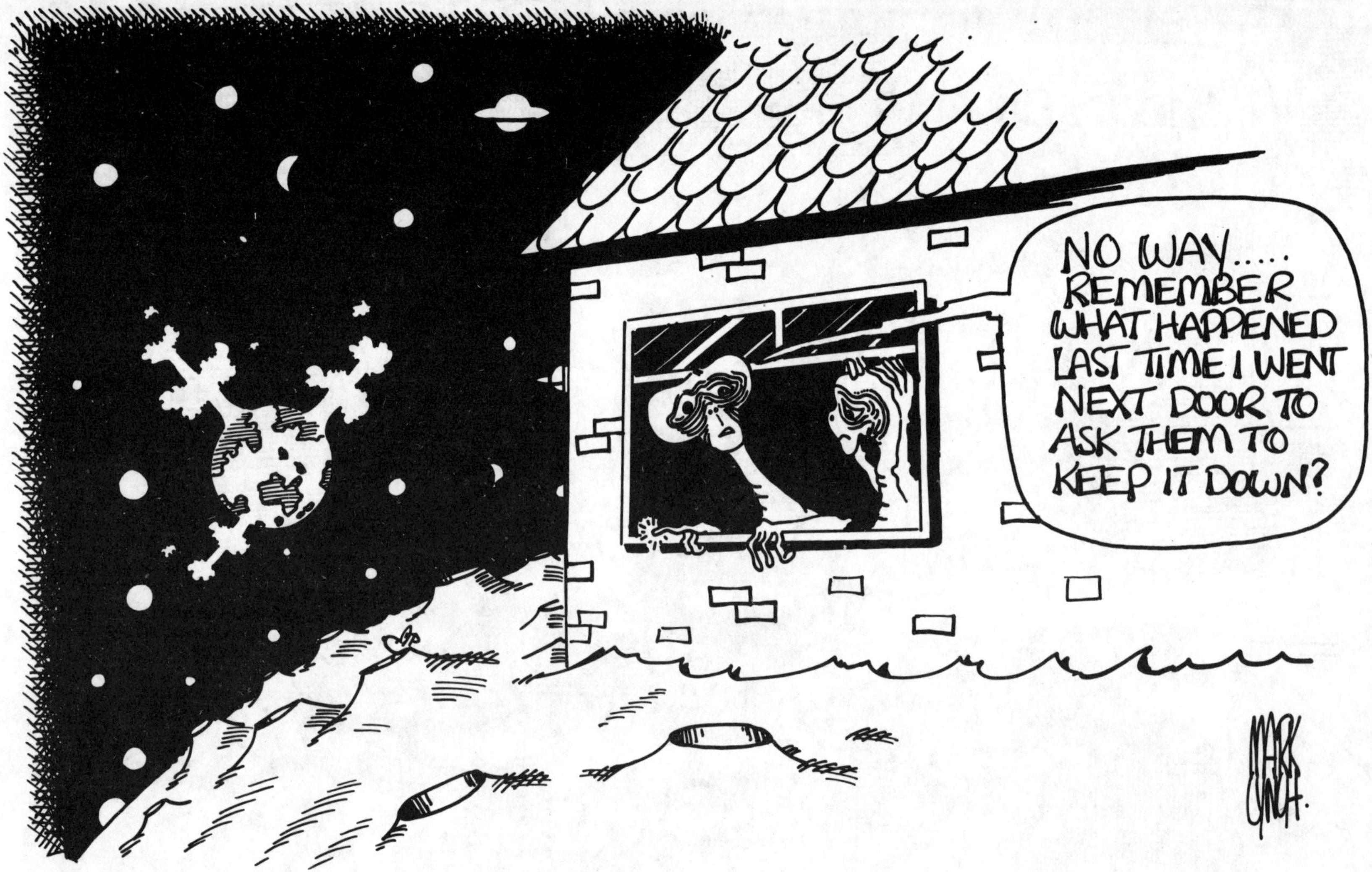
NO WAY..... REMEMBER WHAT HAPPENED LAST TIME I WENT NEXT DOOR TO ASK THEM TO KEEP IT DOWN?
MARK LYNCH.

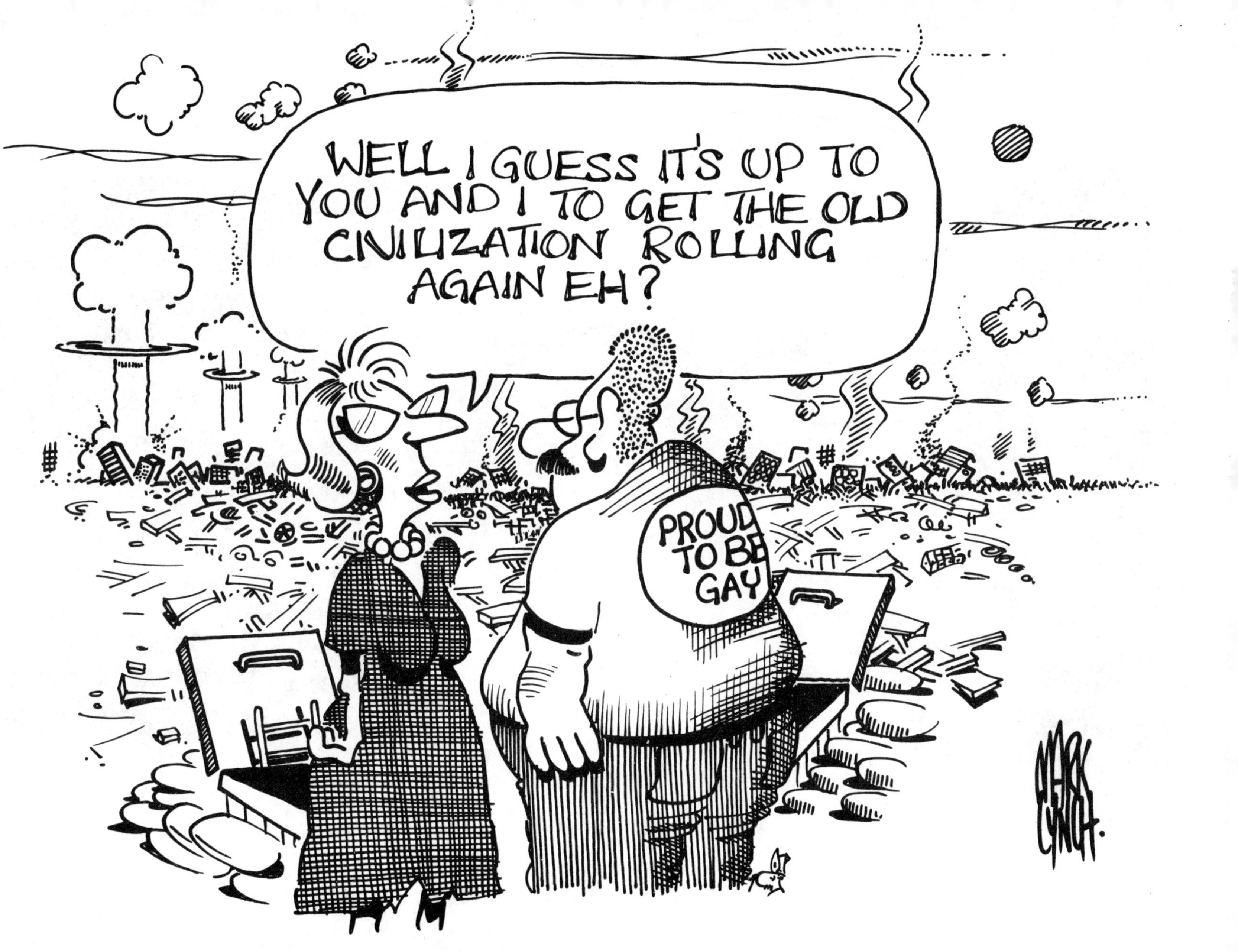
WELL I GUESS IT'S UP TO YOU AND I TO GET THE OLD CIVILIZATION ROLLING AGAIN EH?
PROUD TO BE GAY

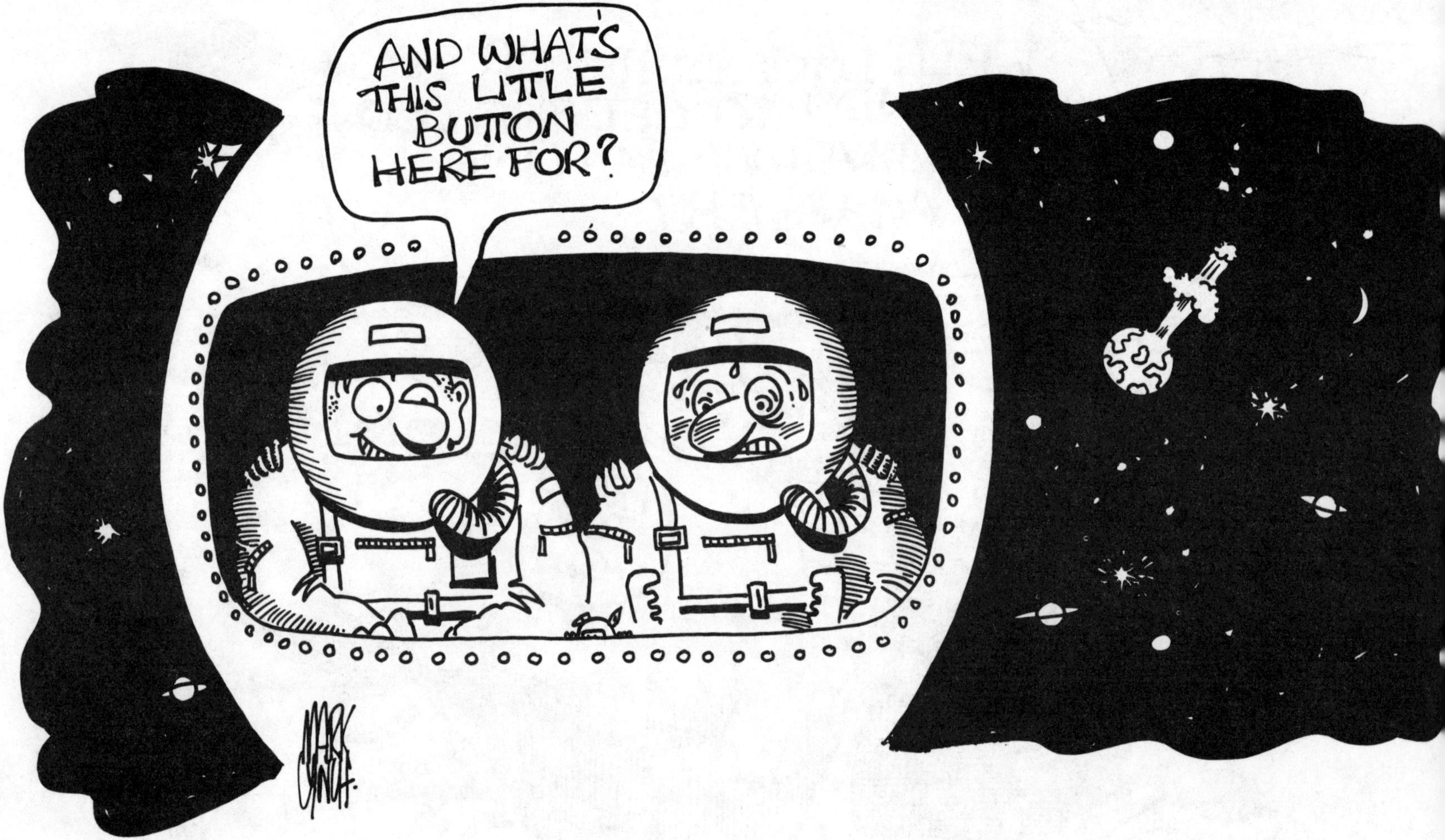
AND WHAT'S THIS LITTLE BUTTON HERE FOR?

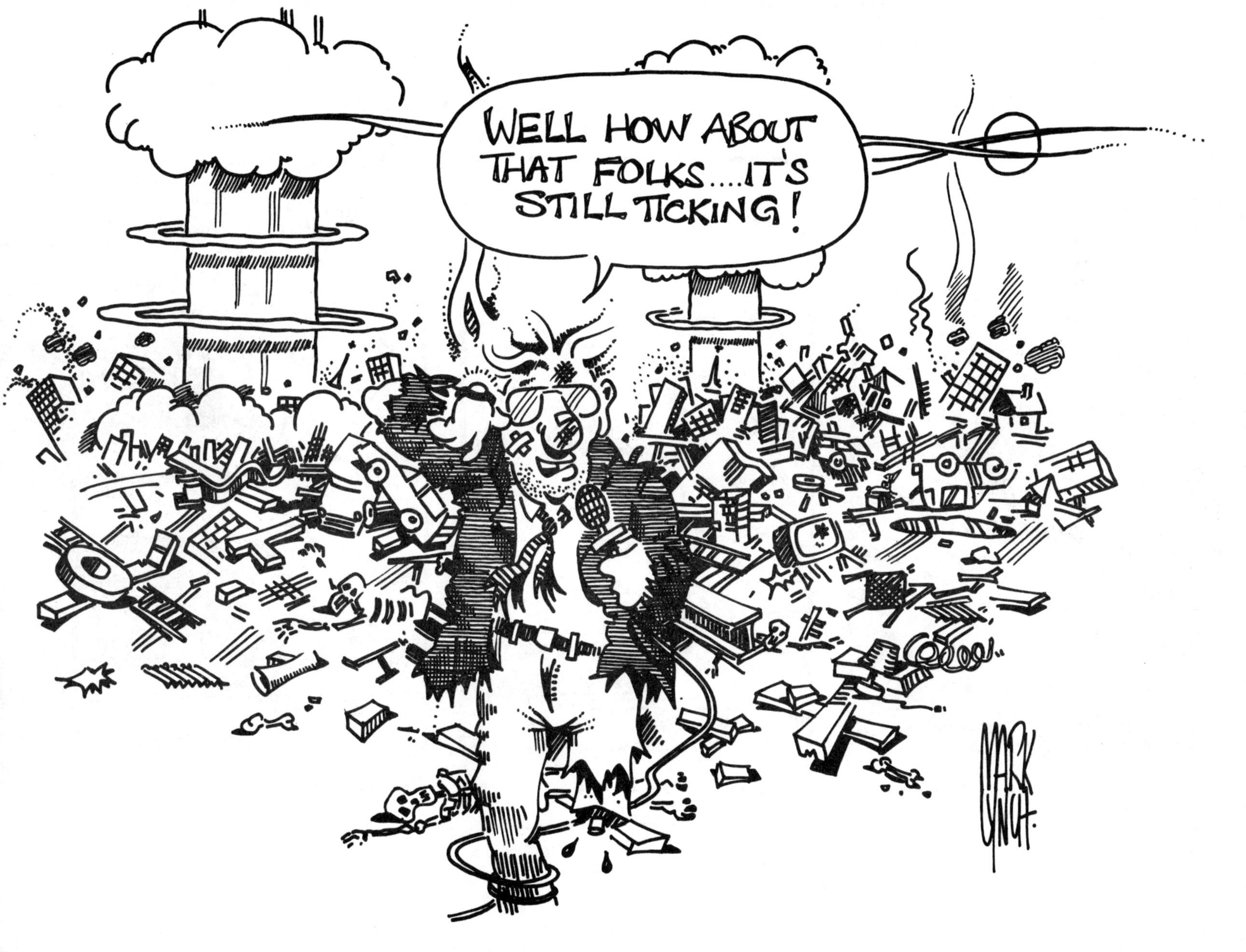
WELL HOW ABOUT THAT FOLKS....IT'S STILL TICKING!
MARK LYNCH.

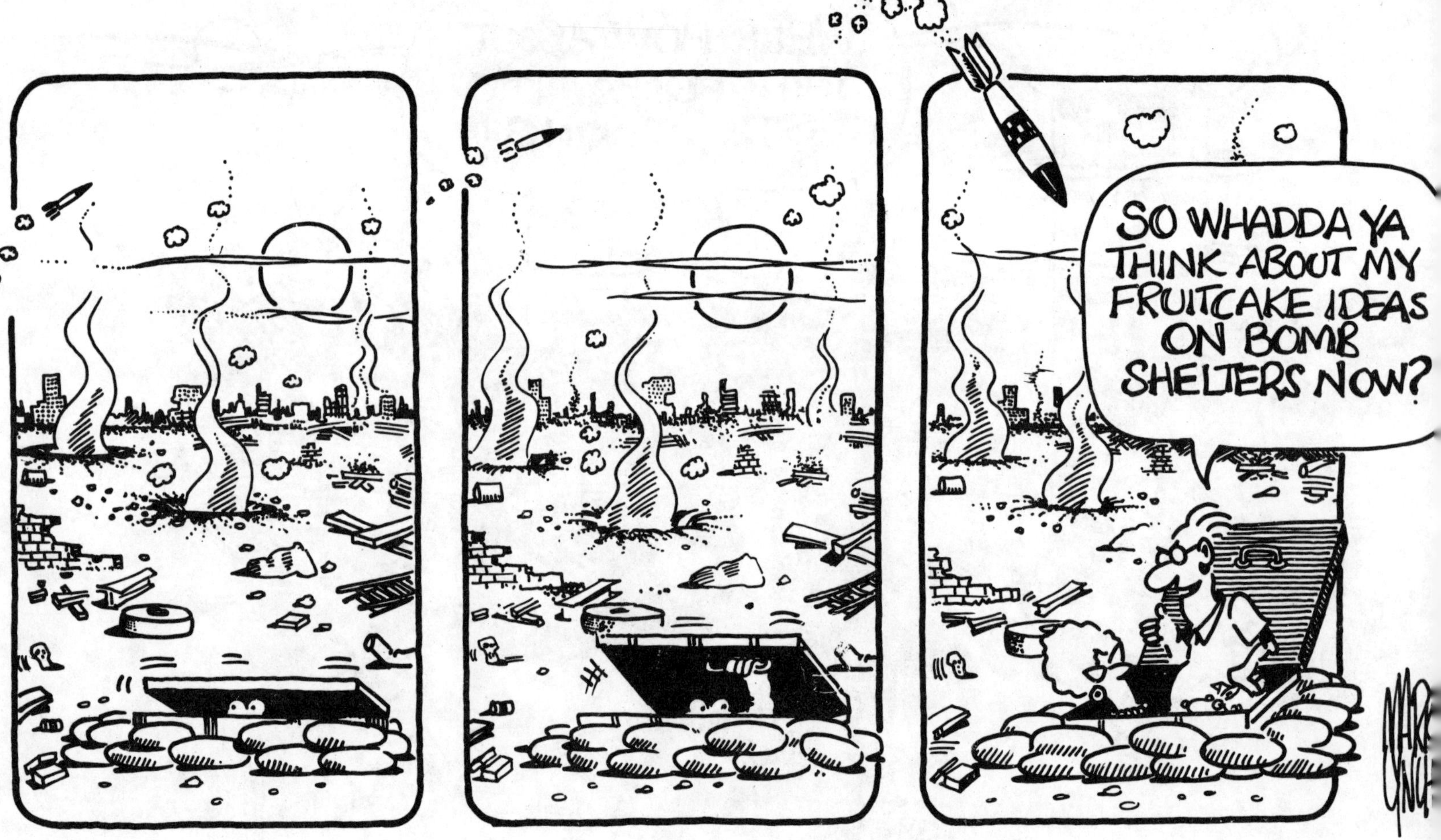
SO WHADDA YA THINK ABOUT MY FRUITCAKE IDEAS ON BOMB SHELTERS NOW?

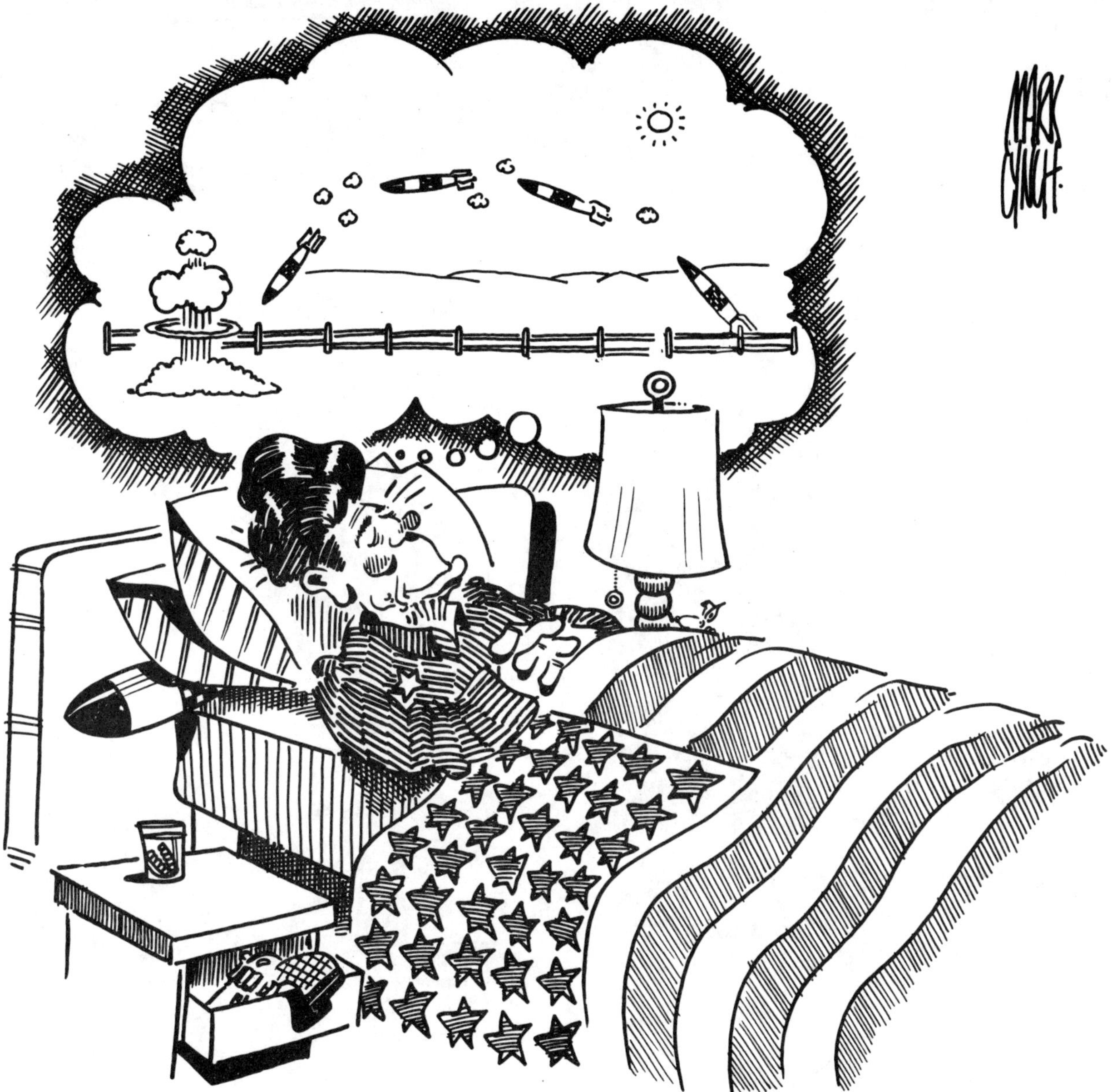

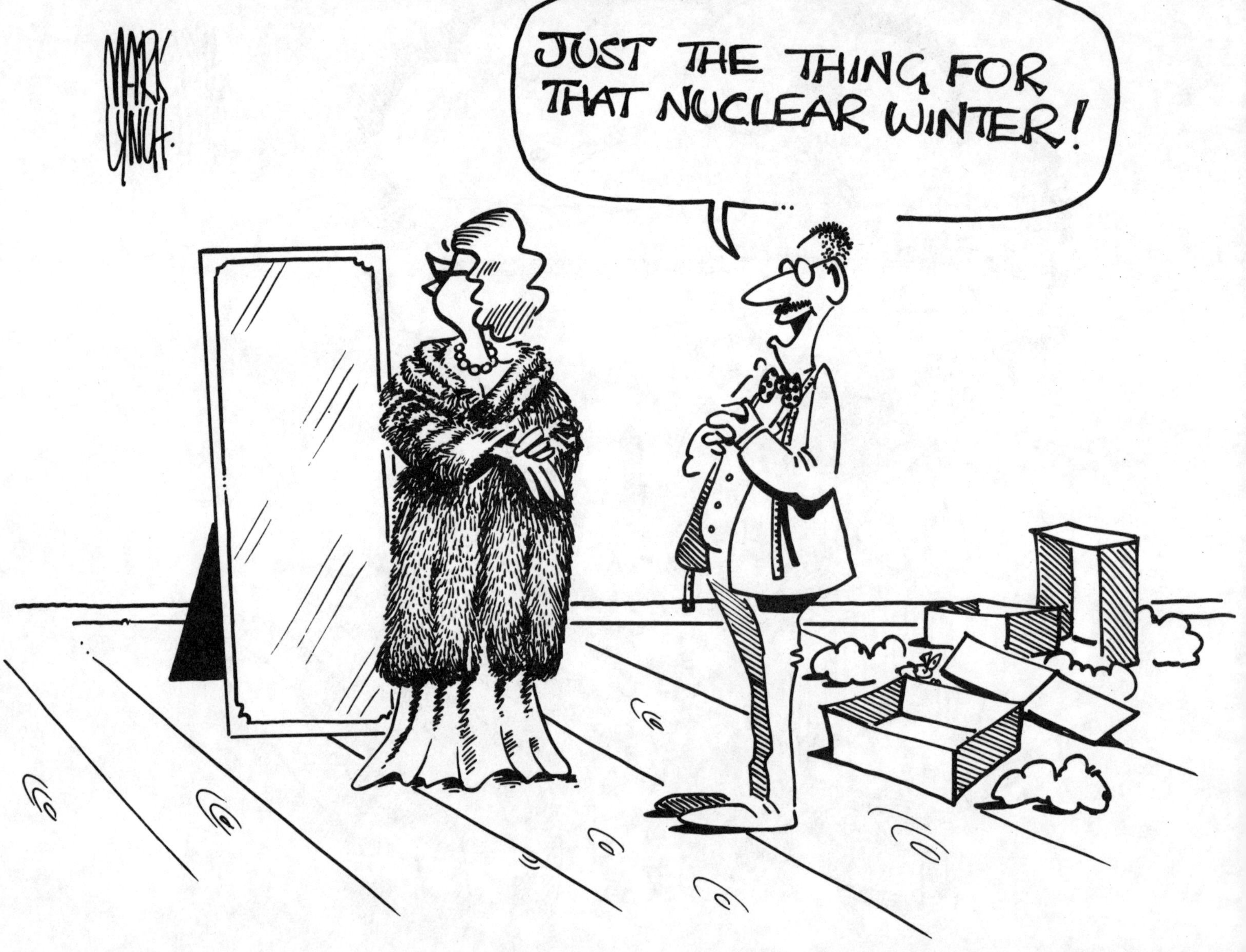
MARK LYNCH.
JUST THE THING FOR THAT NUCLEAR WINTER!

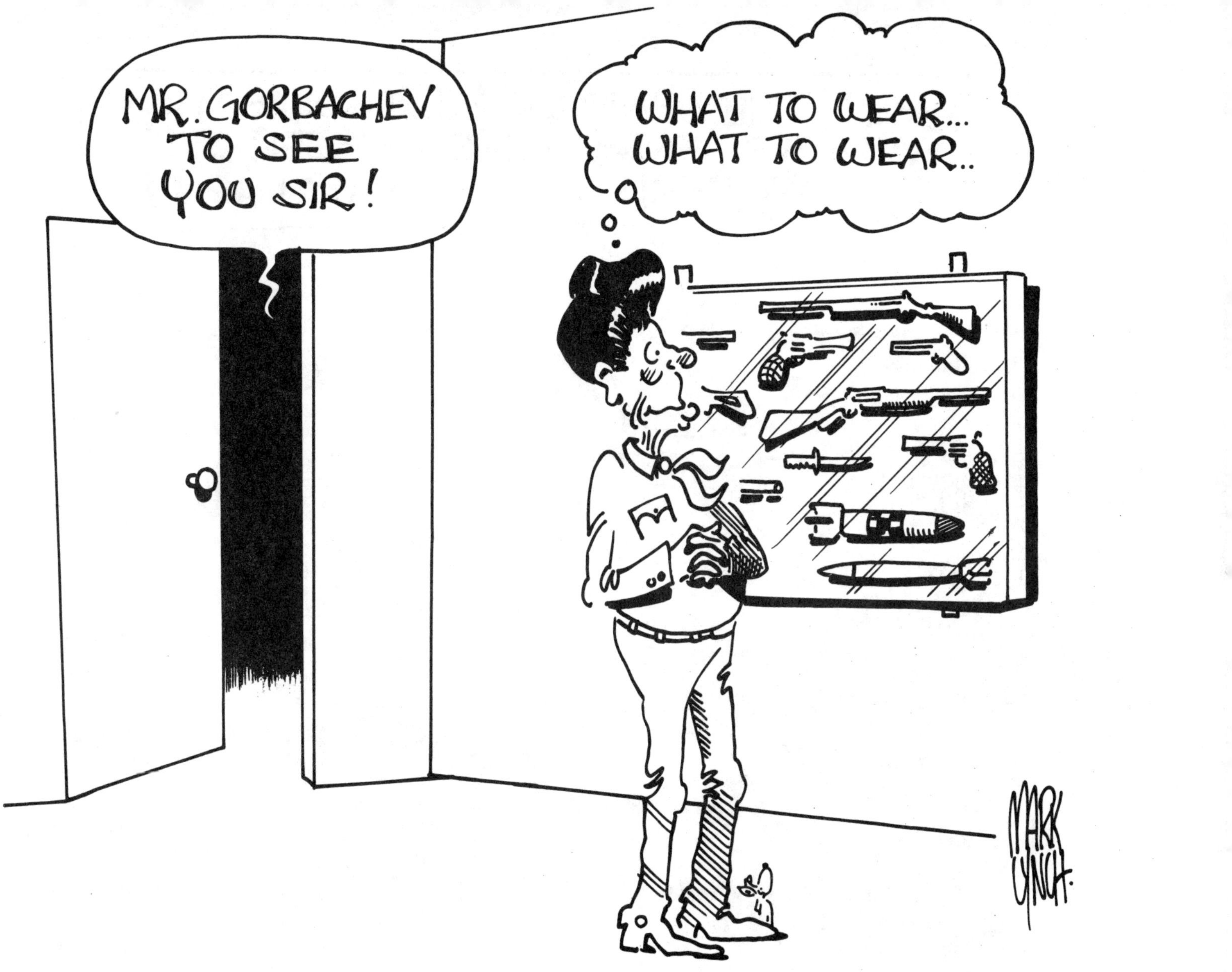
MR. GORBACHEV TO SEE YOU SIR!
WHAT TO WEAR... WHAT TO WEAR..
MARK LYNCH.

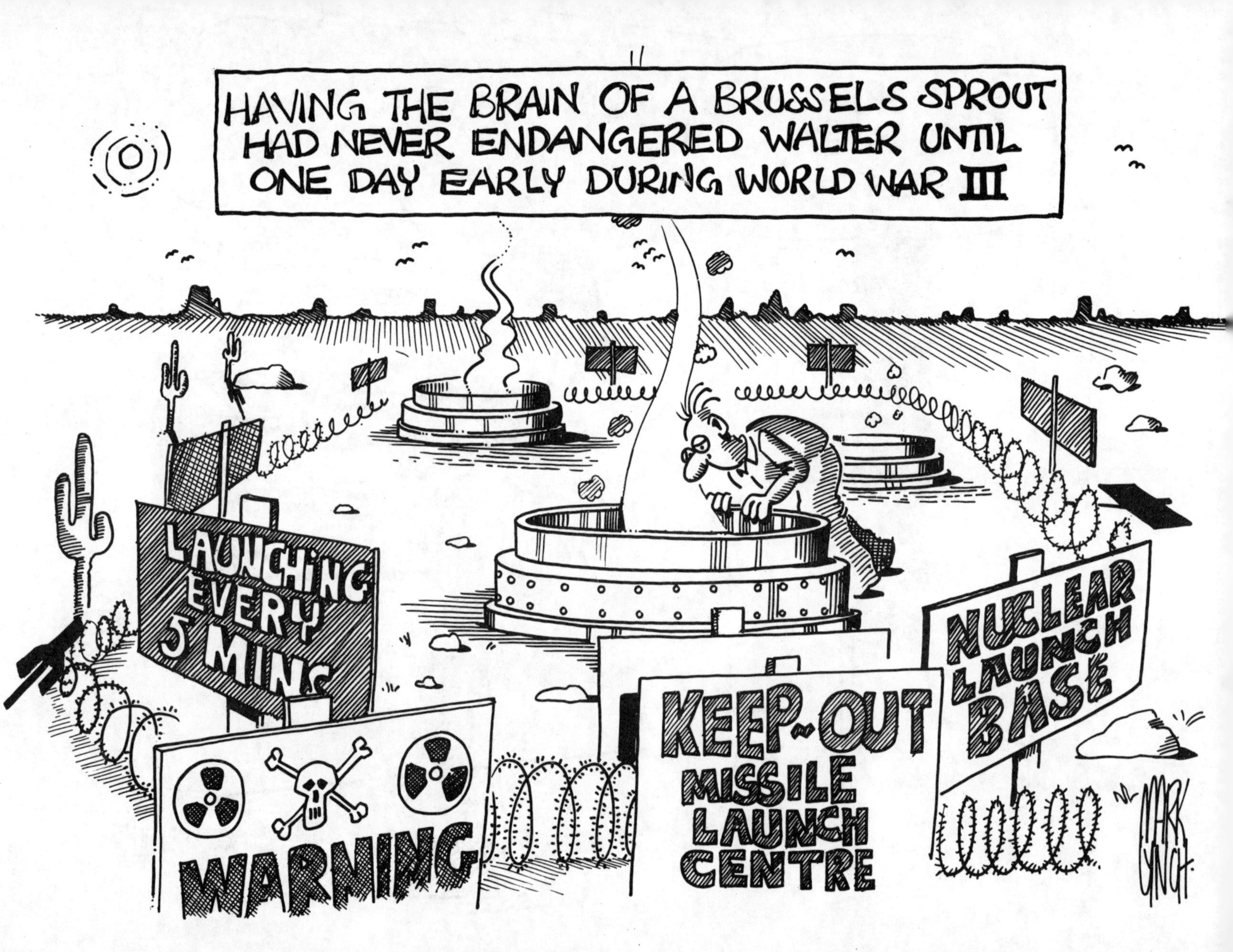
HAVING THE BRAIN OF A BRUSSELS SPROUT HAD NEVER ENDANGERED WALTER UNTIL ONE DAY EARLY DURING WORLD WAR III
LAUNCHING EVERY 5 MINS
NUCLEAR LAUNCH BASE
KEEP-OUT MISSILE LAUNCH CENTRE
WARNING
MARK LYNCH

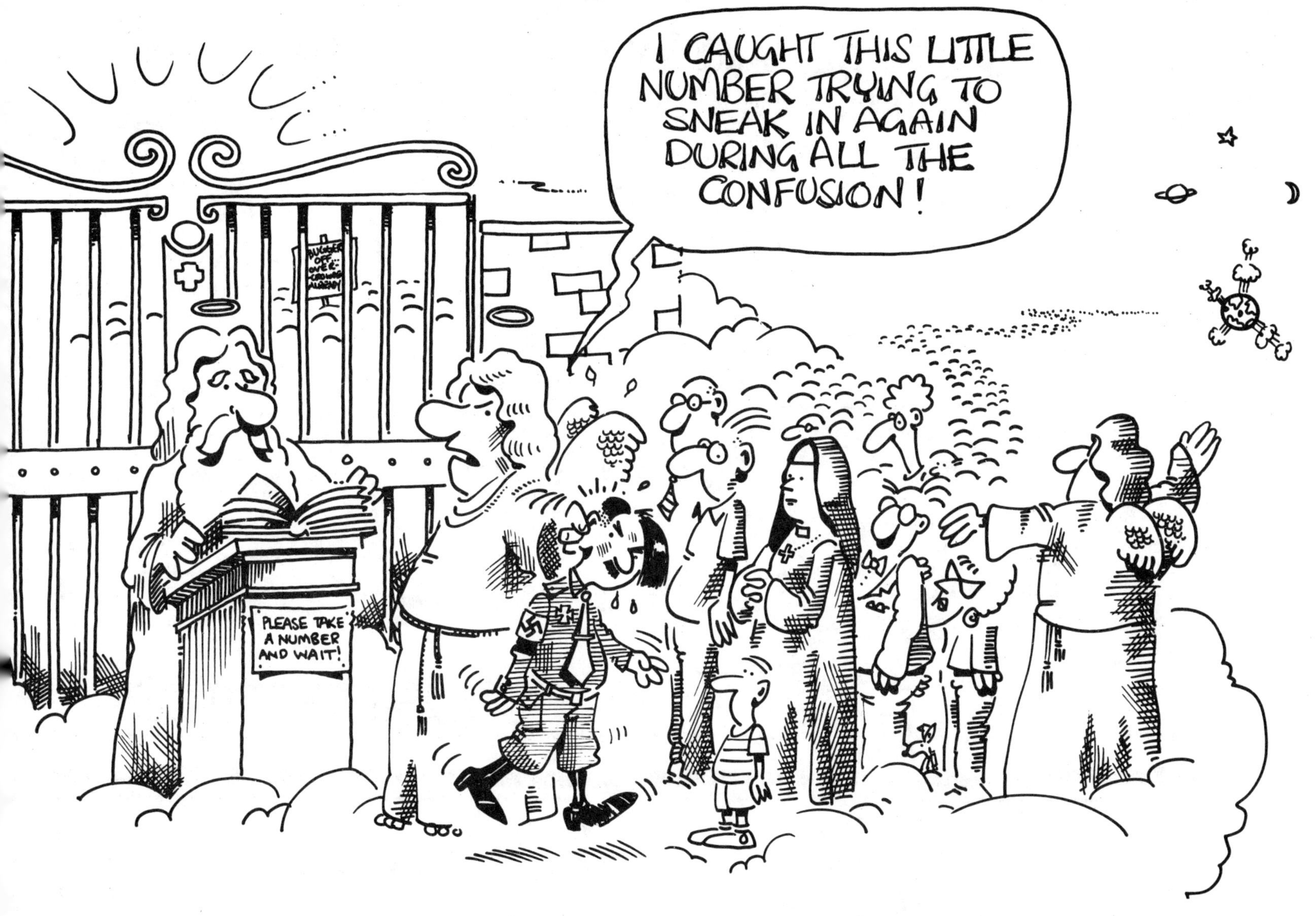
I CAUGHT THIS LITTLE NUMBER TRYING TO SNEAK IN AGAIN DURING ALL THE CONFUSION!
BUGGER OFF... OVER-CROWDED ALREADY
PLEASE TAKE A NUMBER AND WAIT!

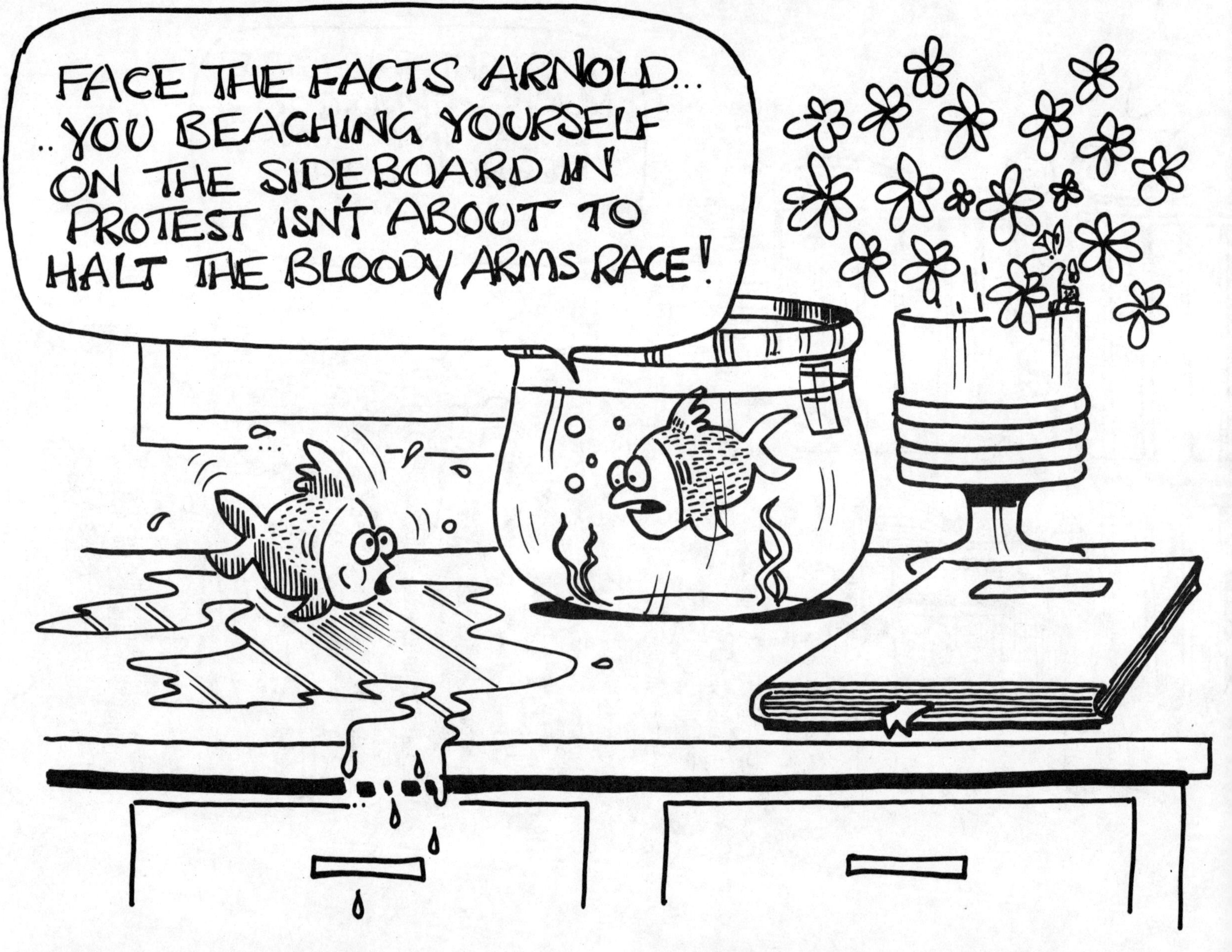
FACE THE FACTS ARNOLD... ..YOU BEACHING YOURSELF ON THE SIDEBOARD IN PROTEST ISN'T ABOUT TO HALT THE BLOODY ARMS RACE!

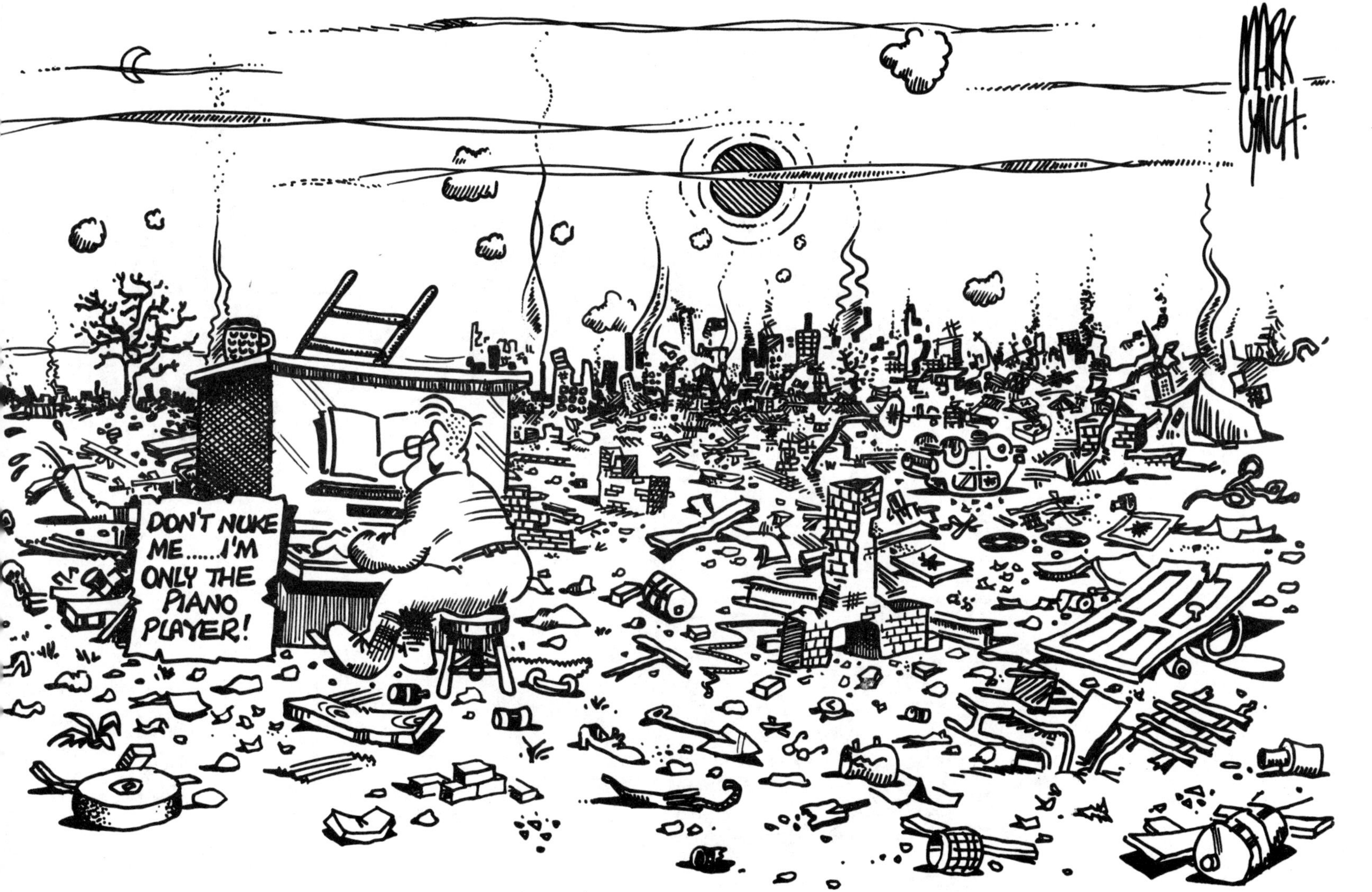
DON'T NUKE ME......I'M ONLY THE PIANO PLAYER!

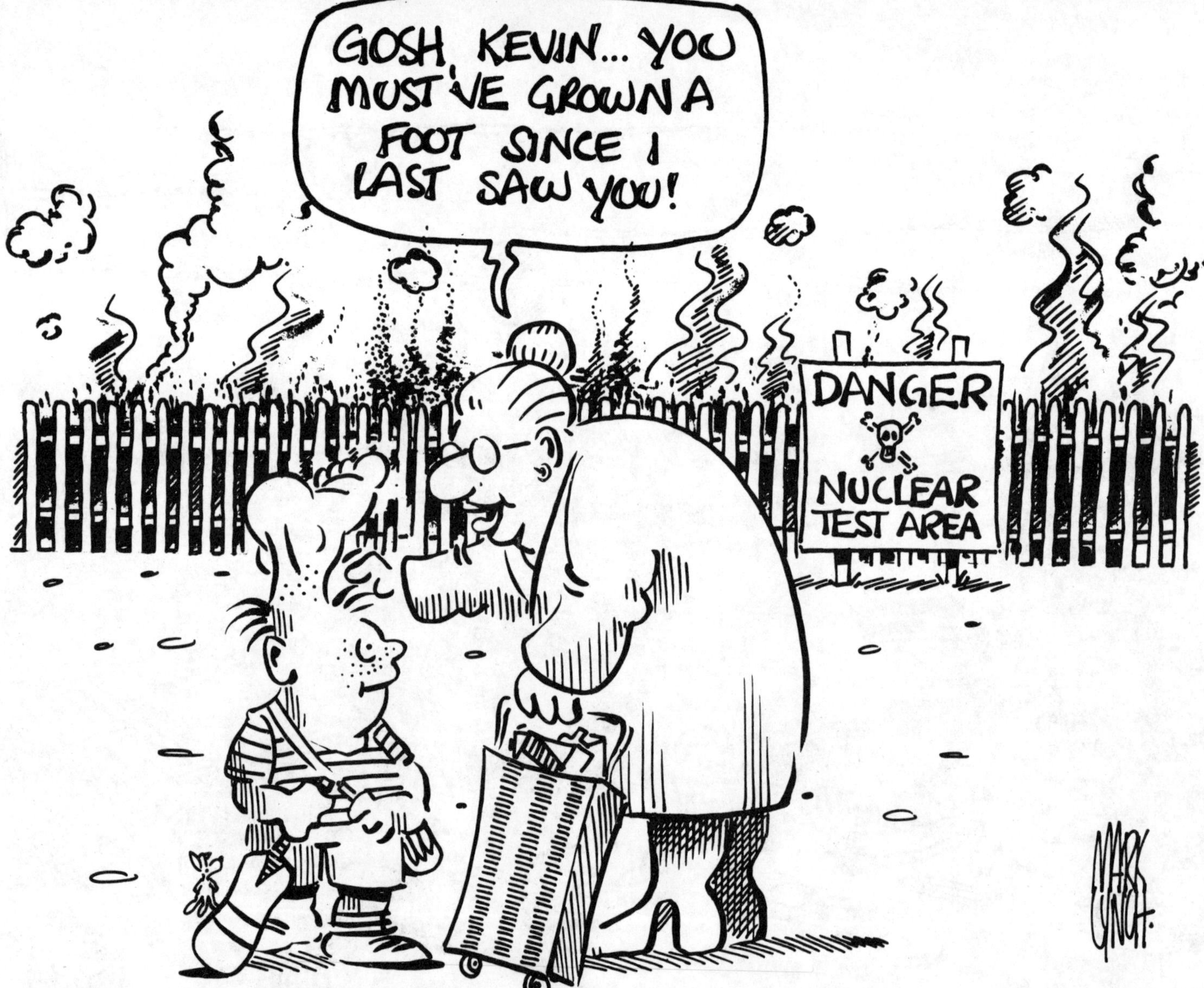
GOSH KEVIN... YOU MUST'VE GROWN A FOOT SINCE I LAST SAW YOU!
DANGER
NUCLEAR TEST AREA
MARK LYNCH.

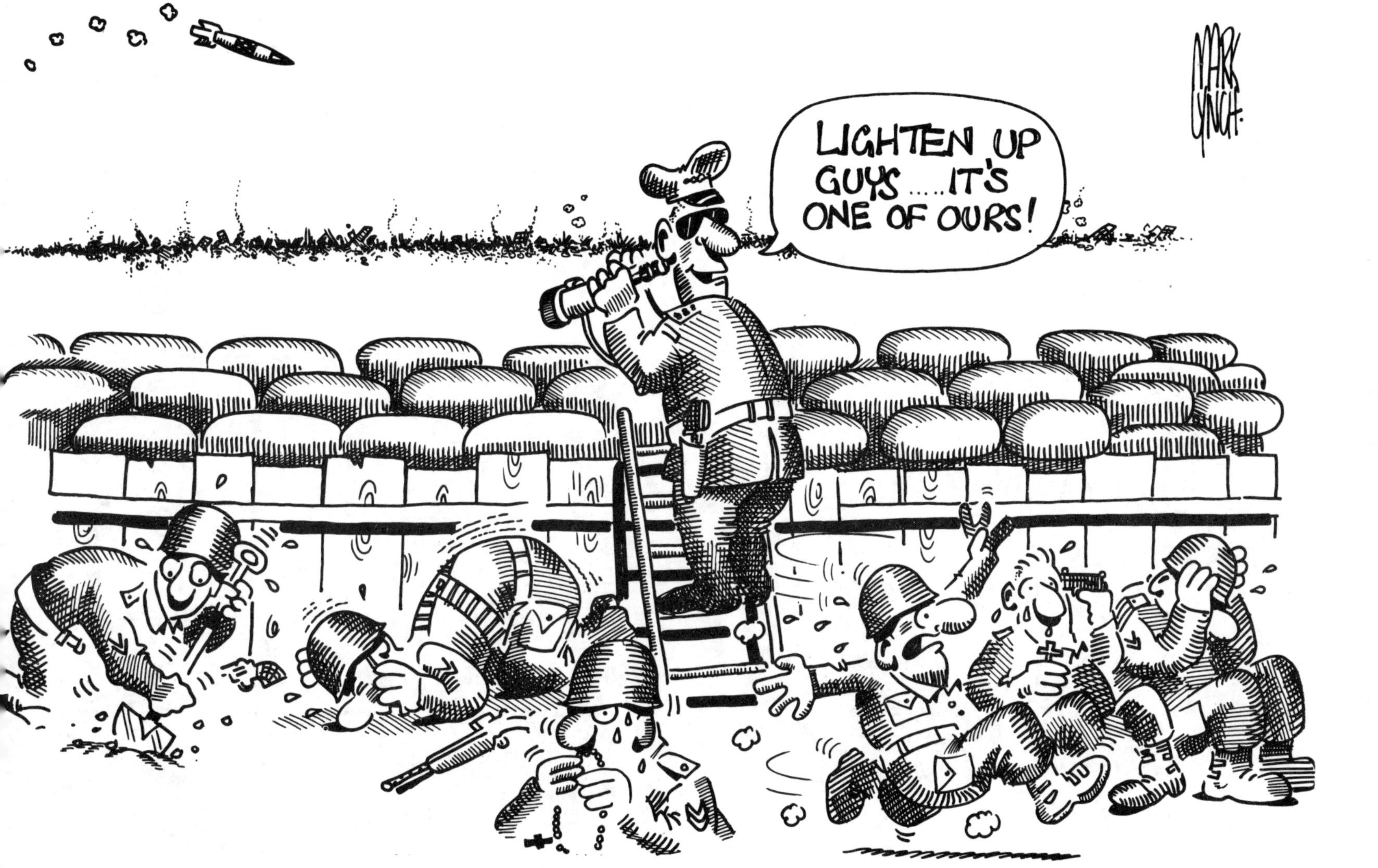
LIGHTEN UP GUYS......IT'S ONE OF OURS!
MARK LYNCH.

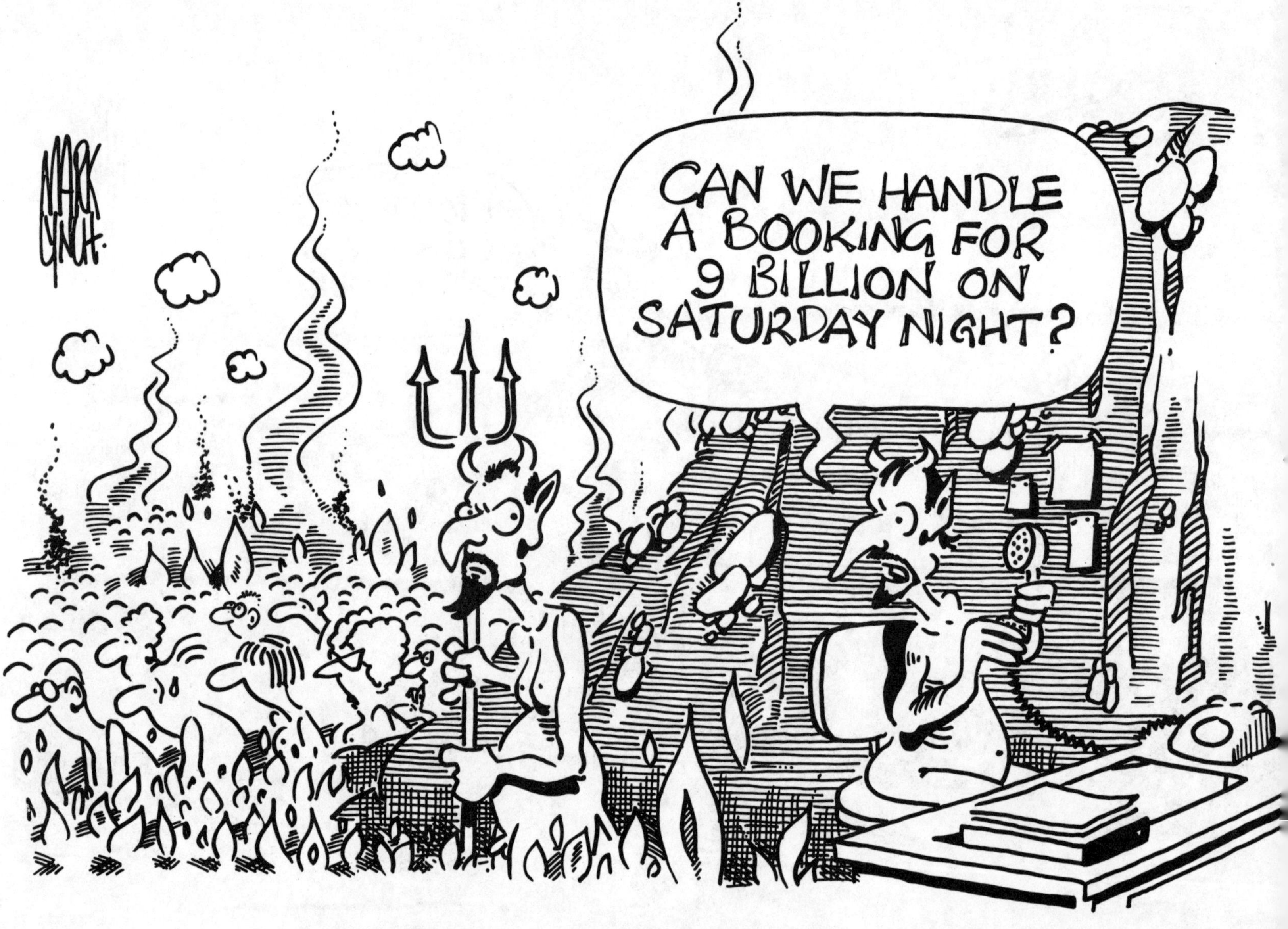
CAN WE HANDLE A BOOKING FOR 9 BILLION ON SATURDAY NIGHT?

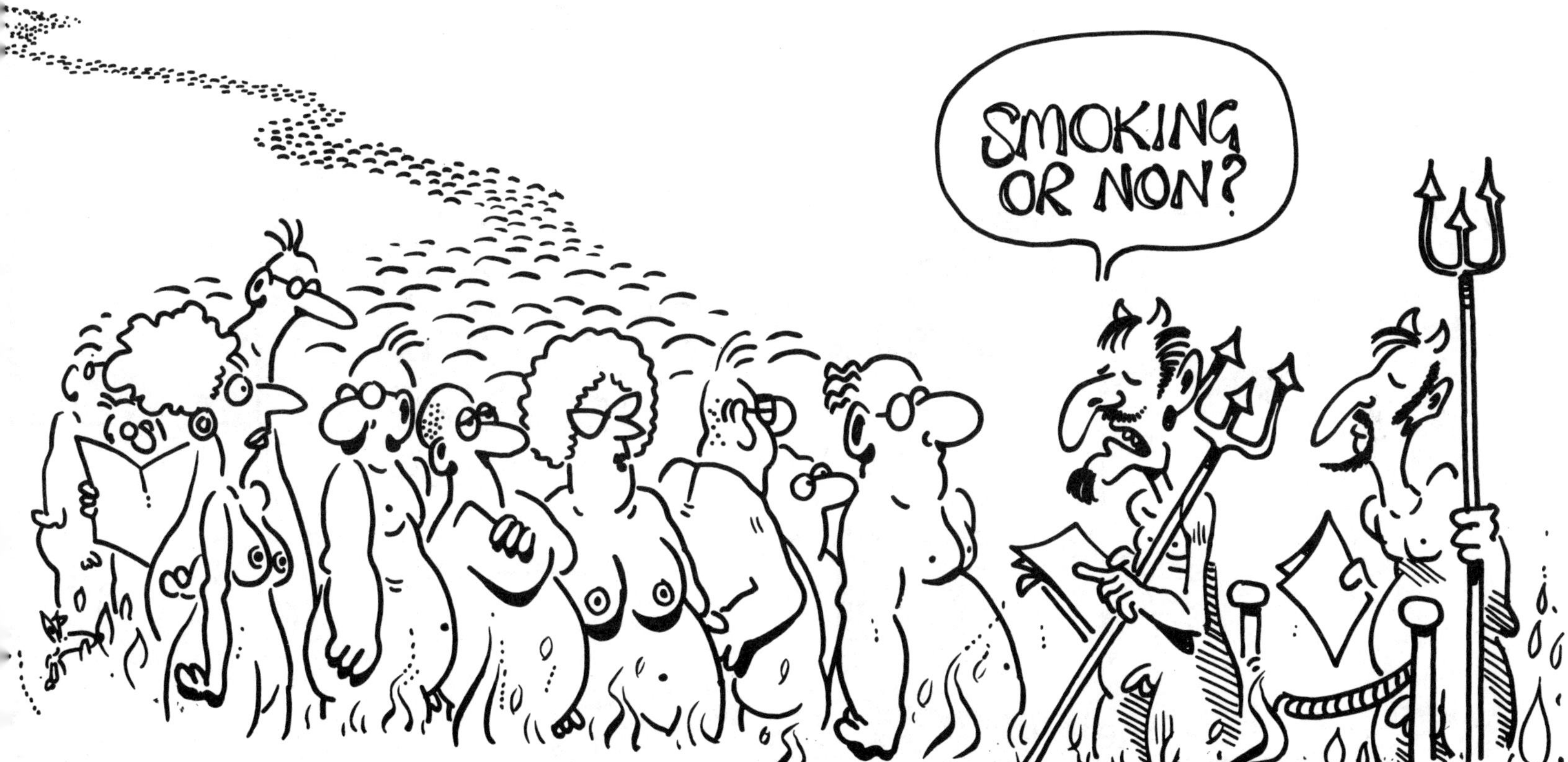
SMOKING
OR NON?

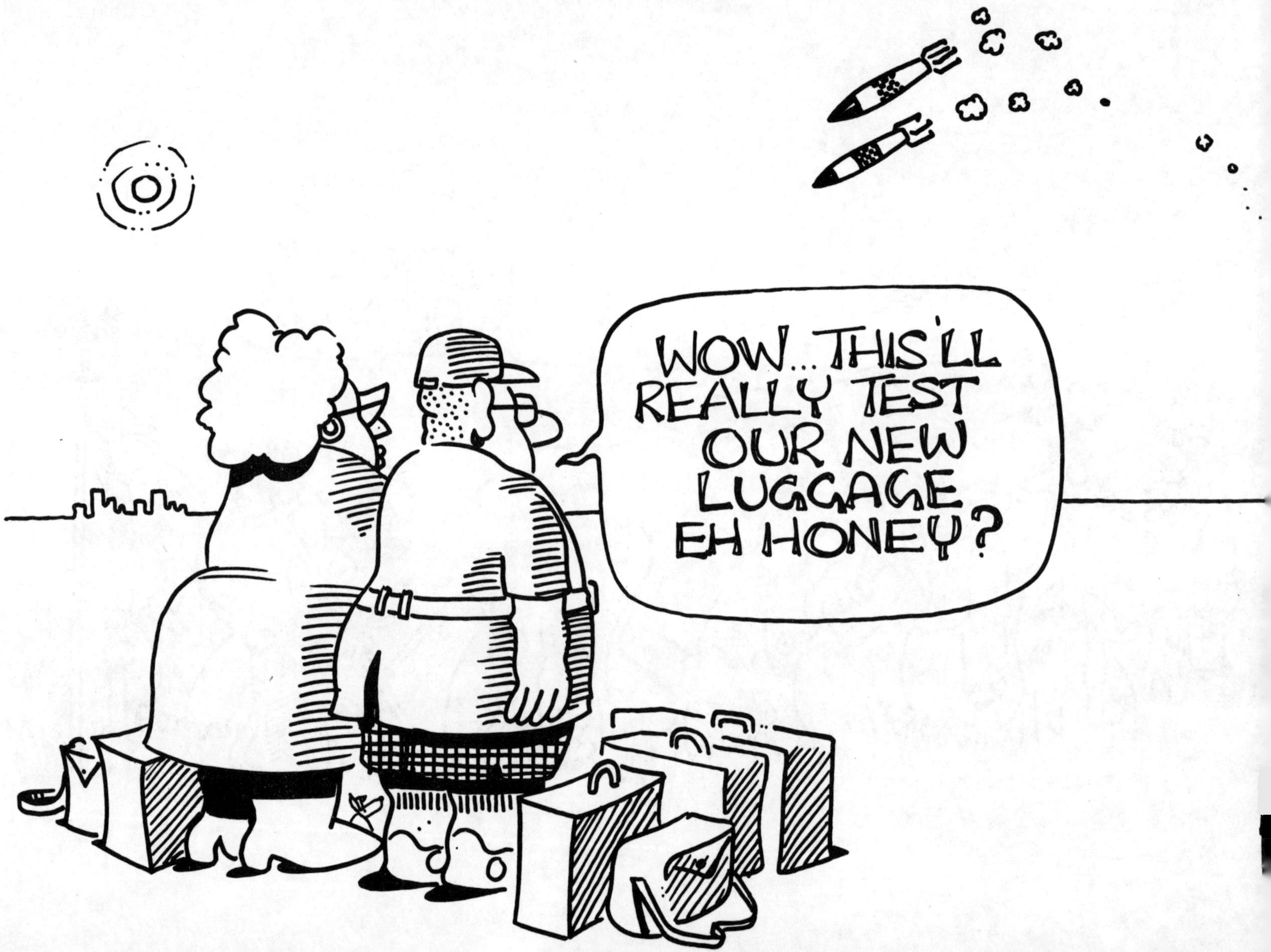
WOW... THIS'LL REALLY TEST OUR NEW LUGGAGE EH HONEY?

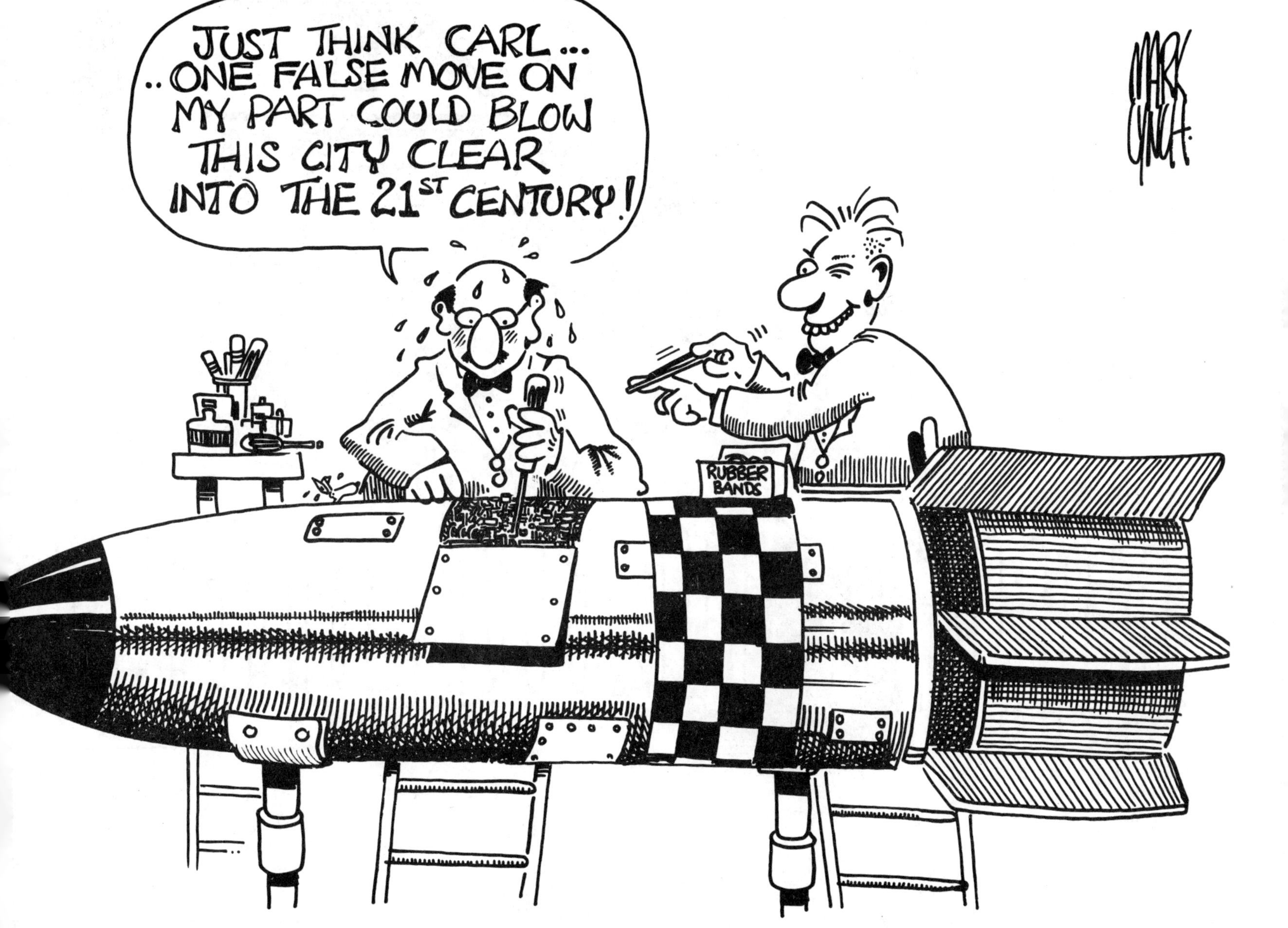
JUST THINK CARL... ..ONE FALSE MOVE ON MY PART COULD BLOW THIS CITY CLEAR INTO THE 21ST CENTURY!
RUBBER BANDS

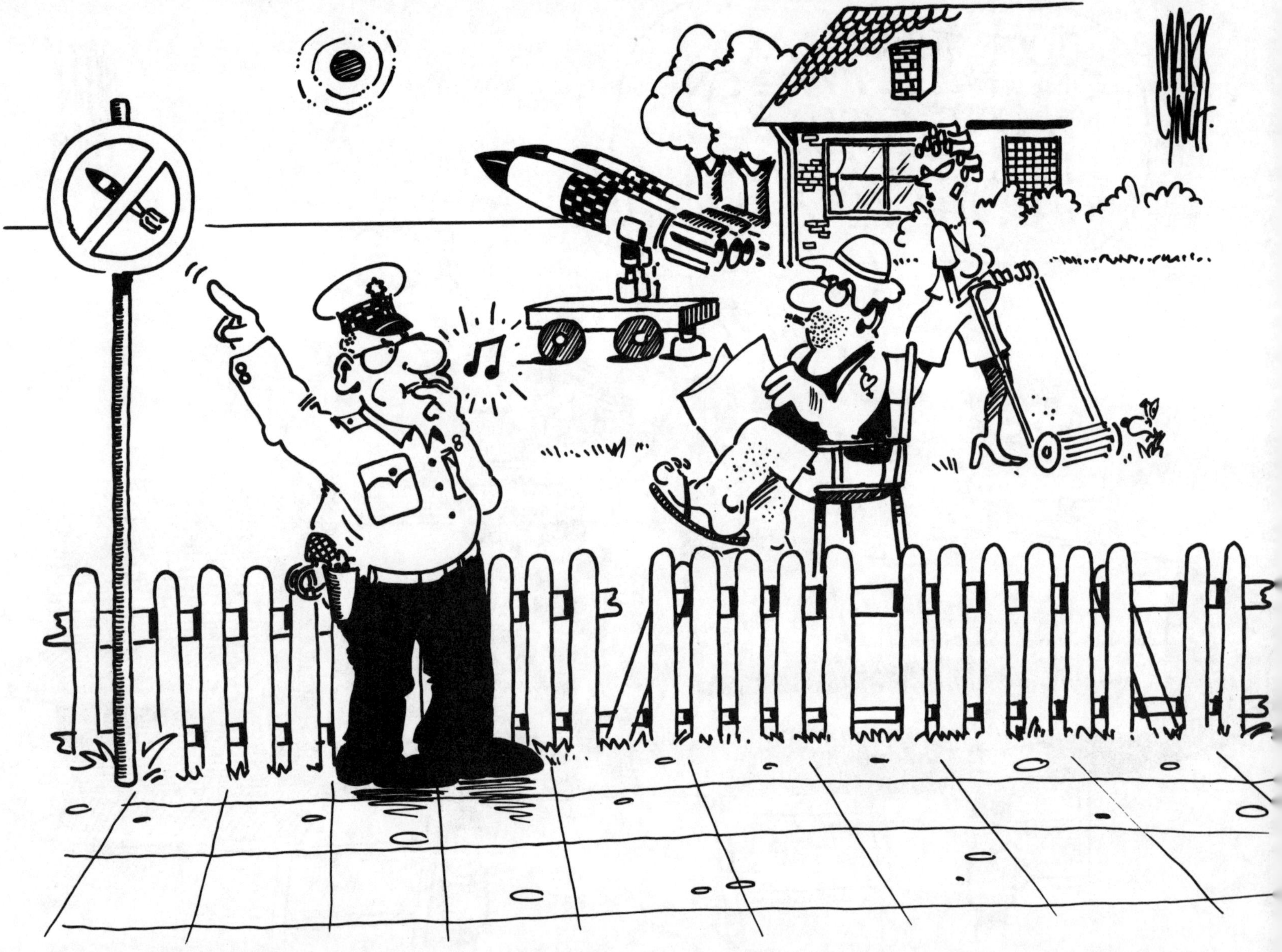
MARK LYNCH.

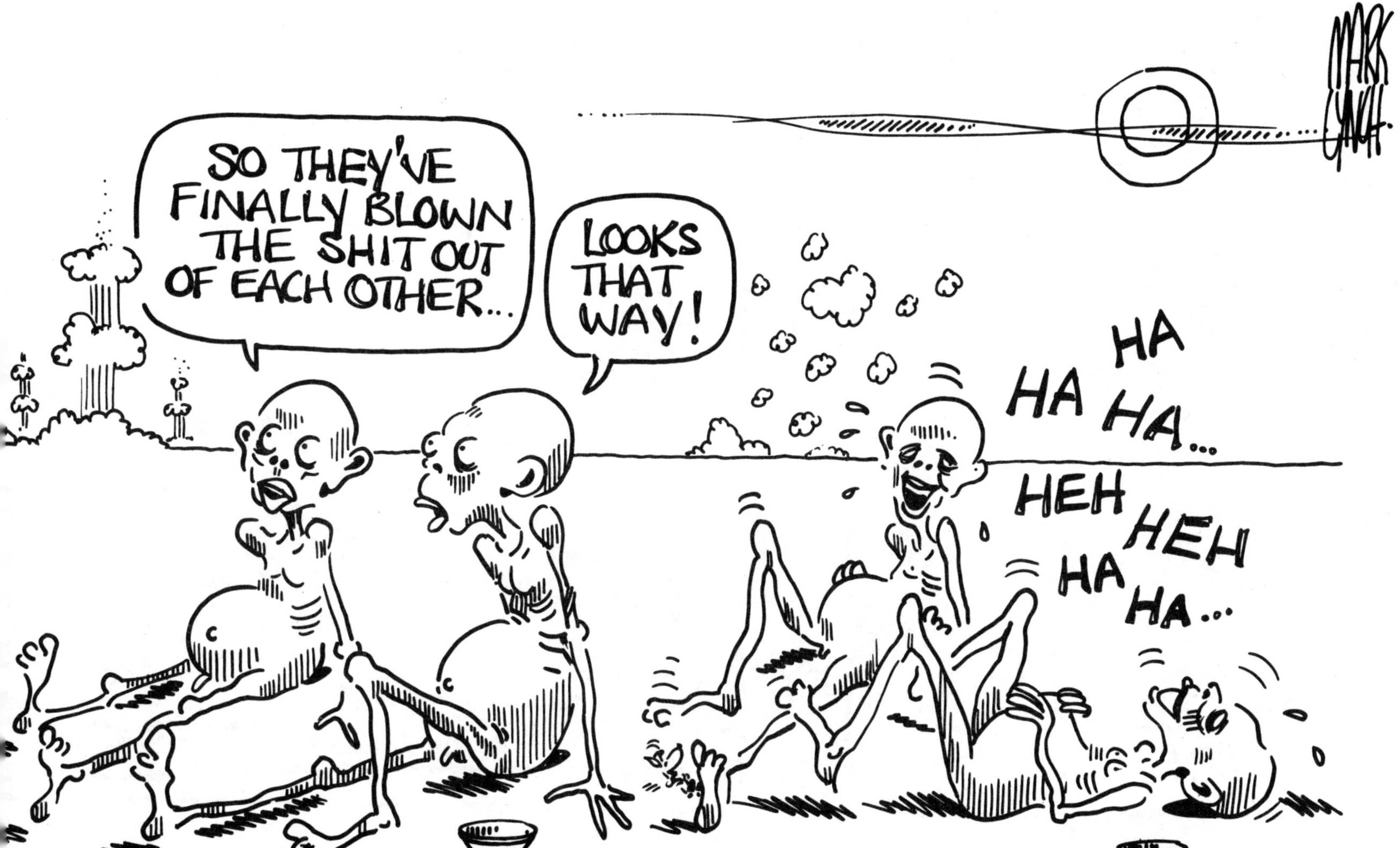
SO THEY'VE FINALLY BLOWN THE SHIT OUT OF EACH OTHER...
LOOKS THAT WAY!
HA HA HA...
HA
HEH HEH
HA HA...
MARK LYNCH

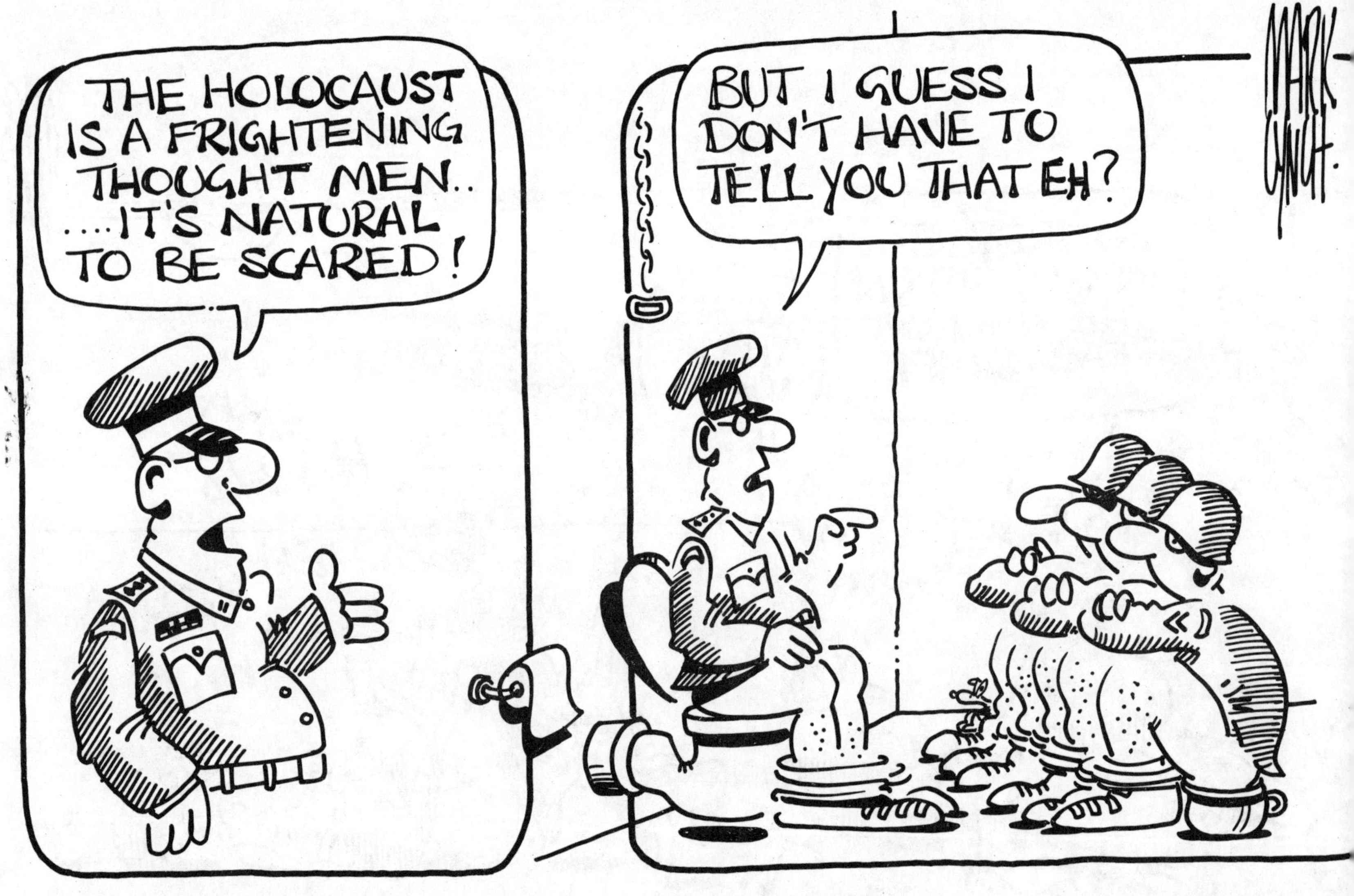
THE HOLOCAUST IS A FRIGHTENING THOUGHT MEN.. ....IT'S NATURAL TO BE SCARED!
BUT I GUESS I DON'T HAVE TO TELL YOU THAT EH?

IT IS AT LEAST COMFORTING TO KNOW THAT OUR NATO ALLIES ARE ON CONSTANT ALERT!

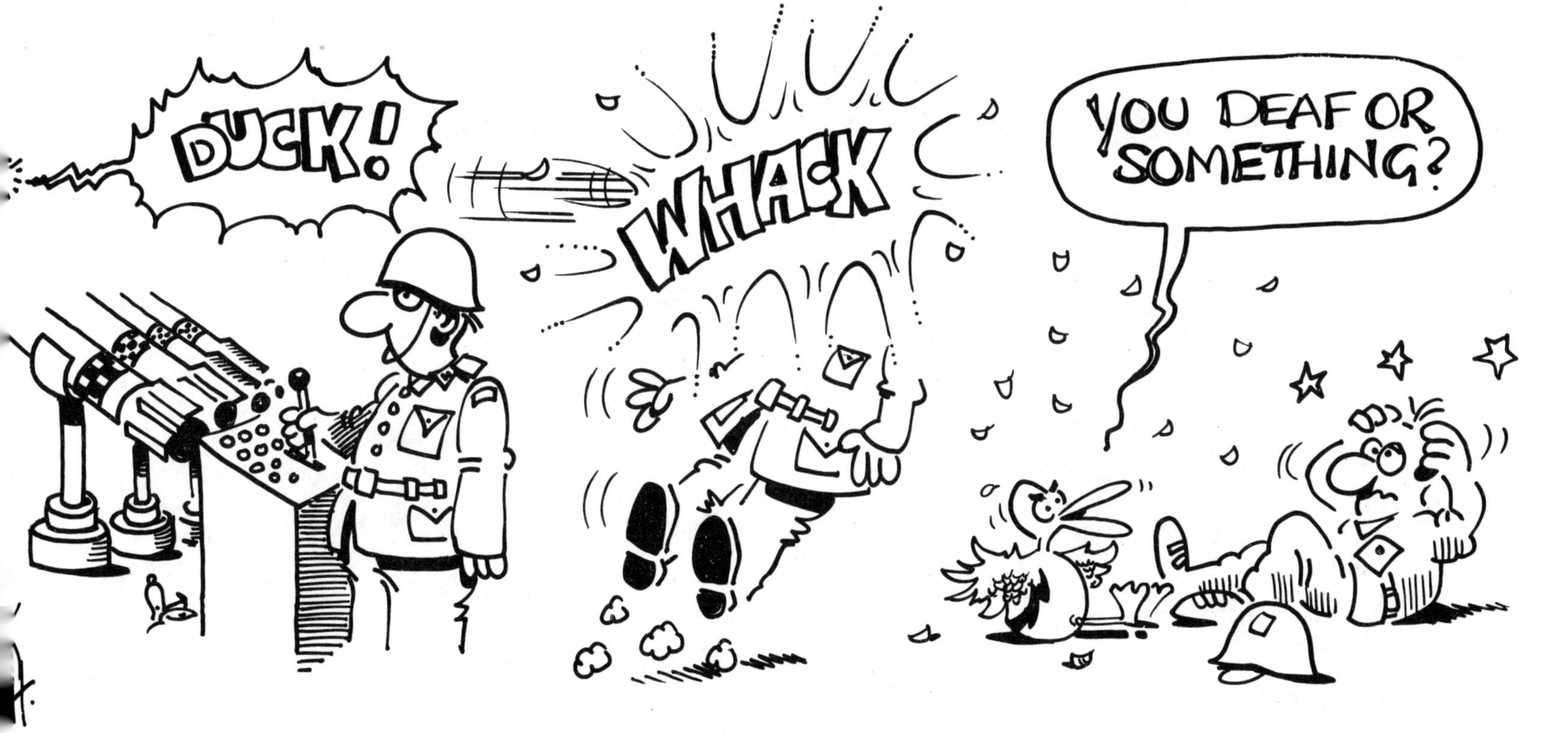
DUCK!
WHACK
YOU DEAF OR SOMETHING?

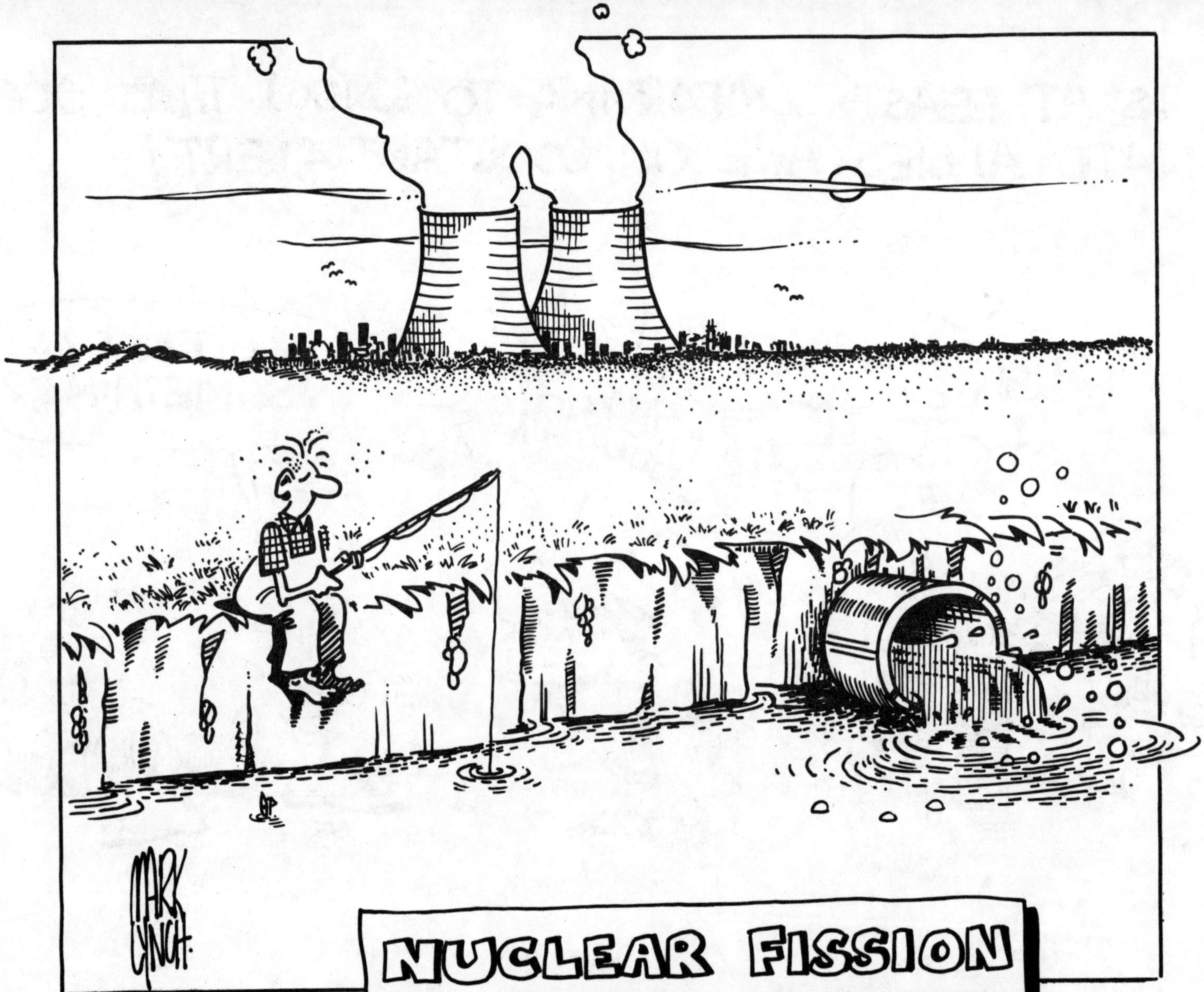
MARK LYNCH.
NUCLEAR FISSION

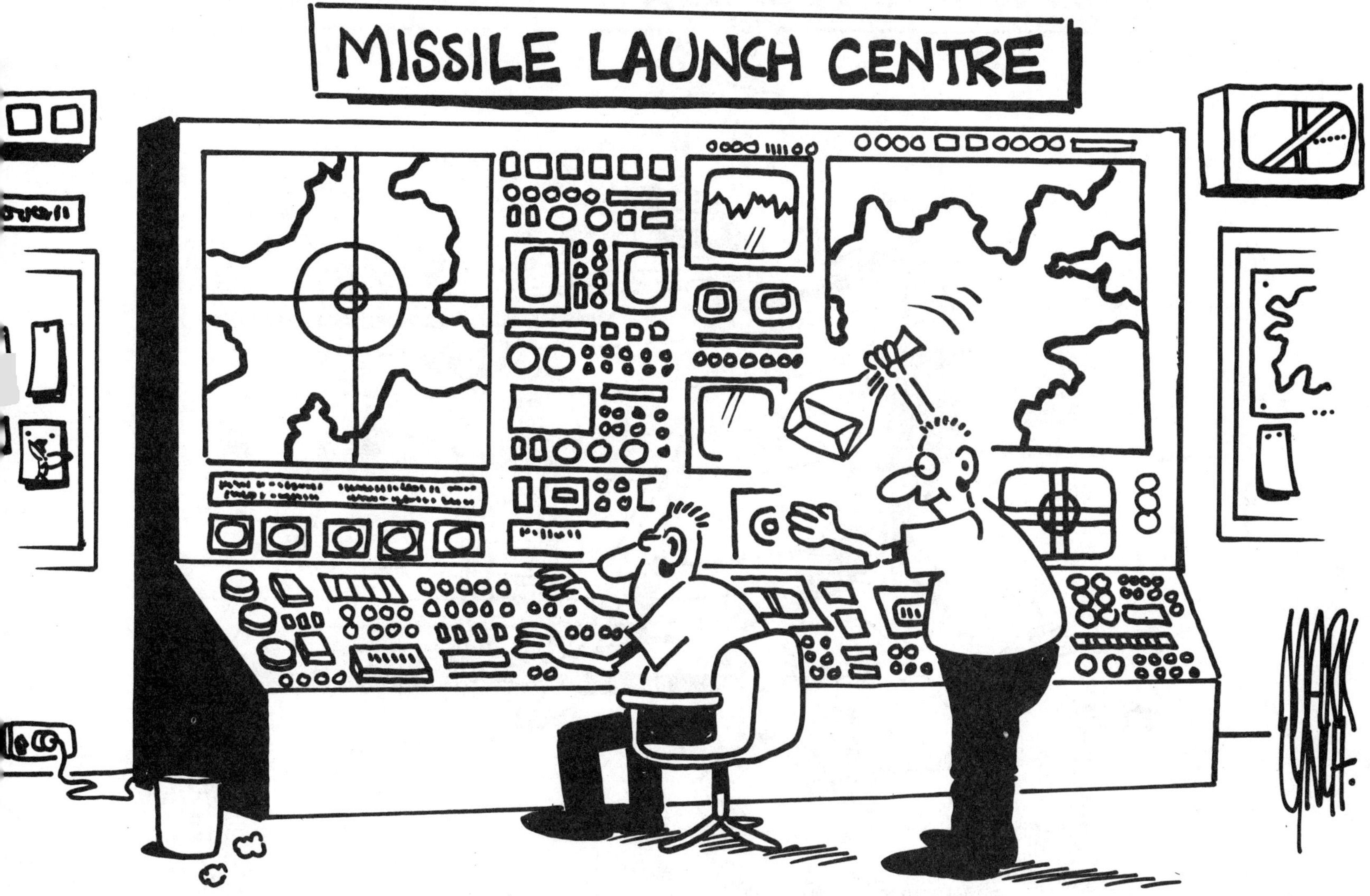
MISSILE LAUNCH CENTRE

THE WORLD'S FIRST EARLY WARNING SYSTEM

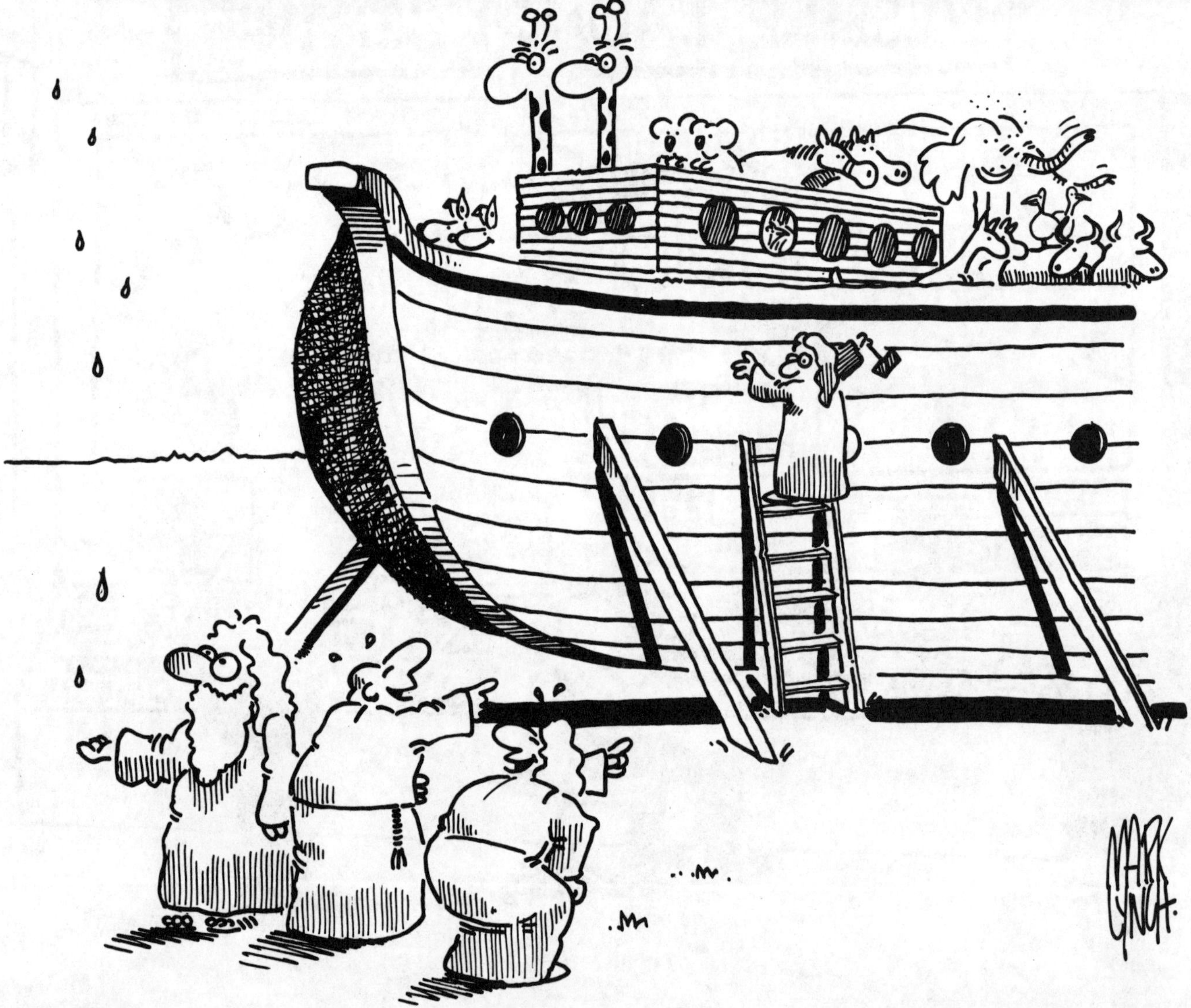
MARK LYNCH

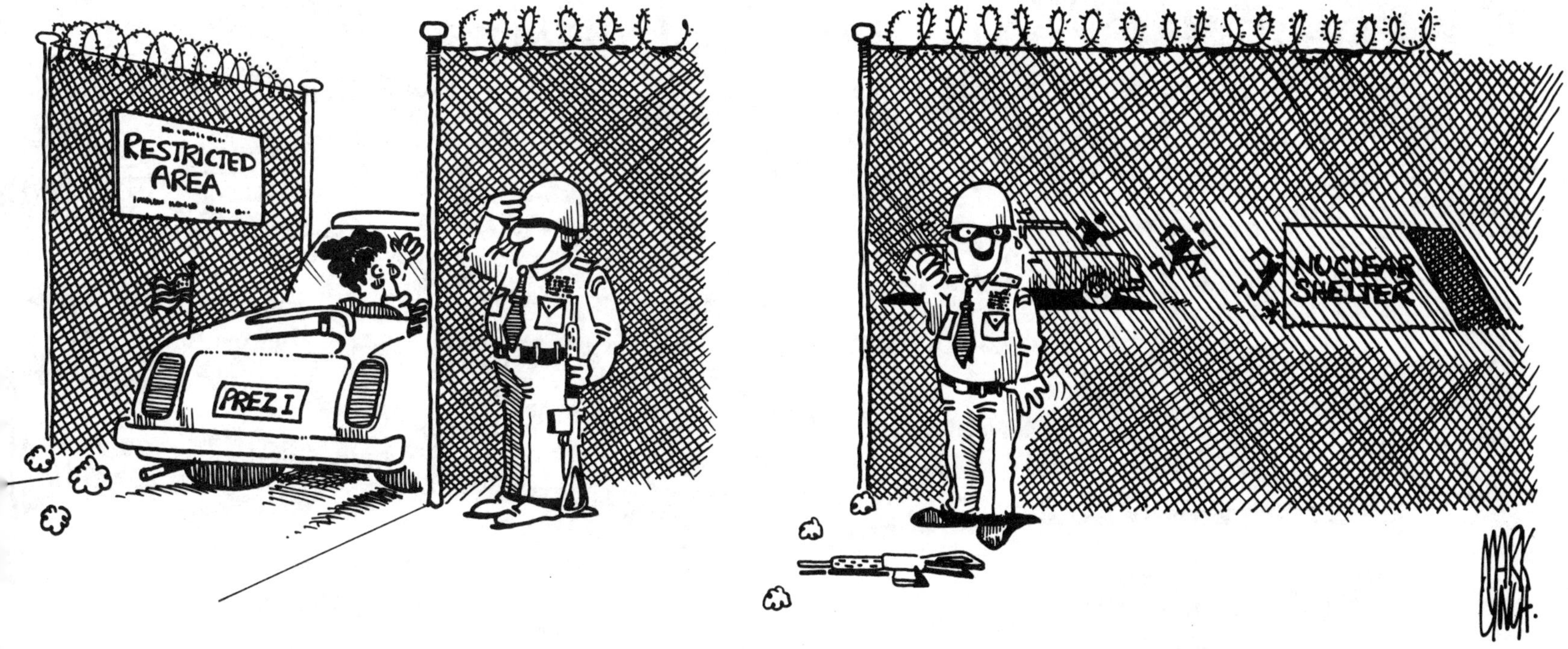
RESTRICTED AREA
PREZ I
NUCLEAR SHELTER
MARK LYNCH.

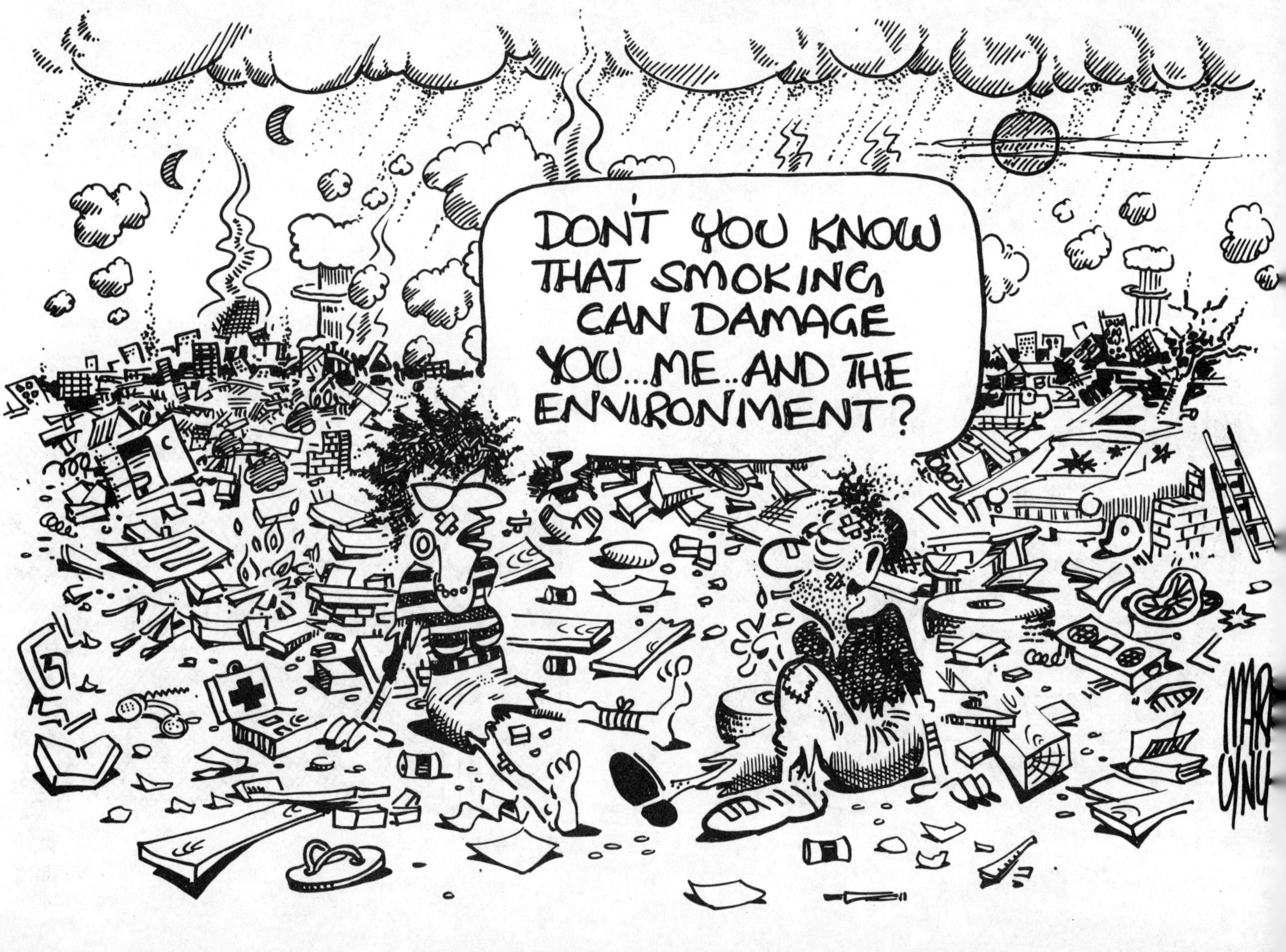
DON'T YOU KNOW THAT SMOKING CAN DAMAGE YOU...ME..AND THE ENVIRONMENT?

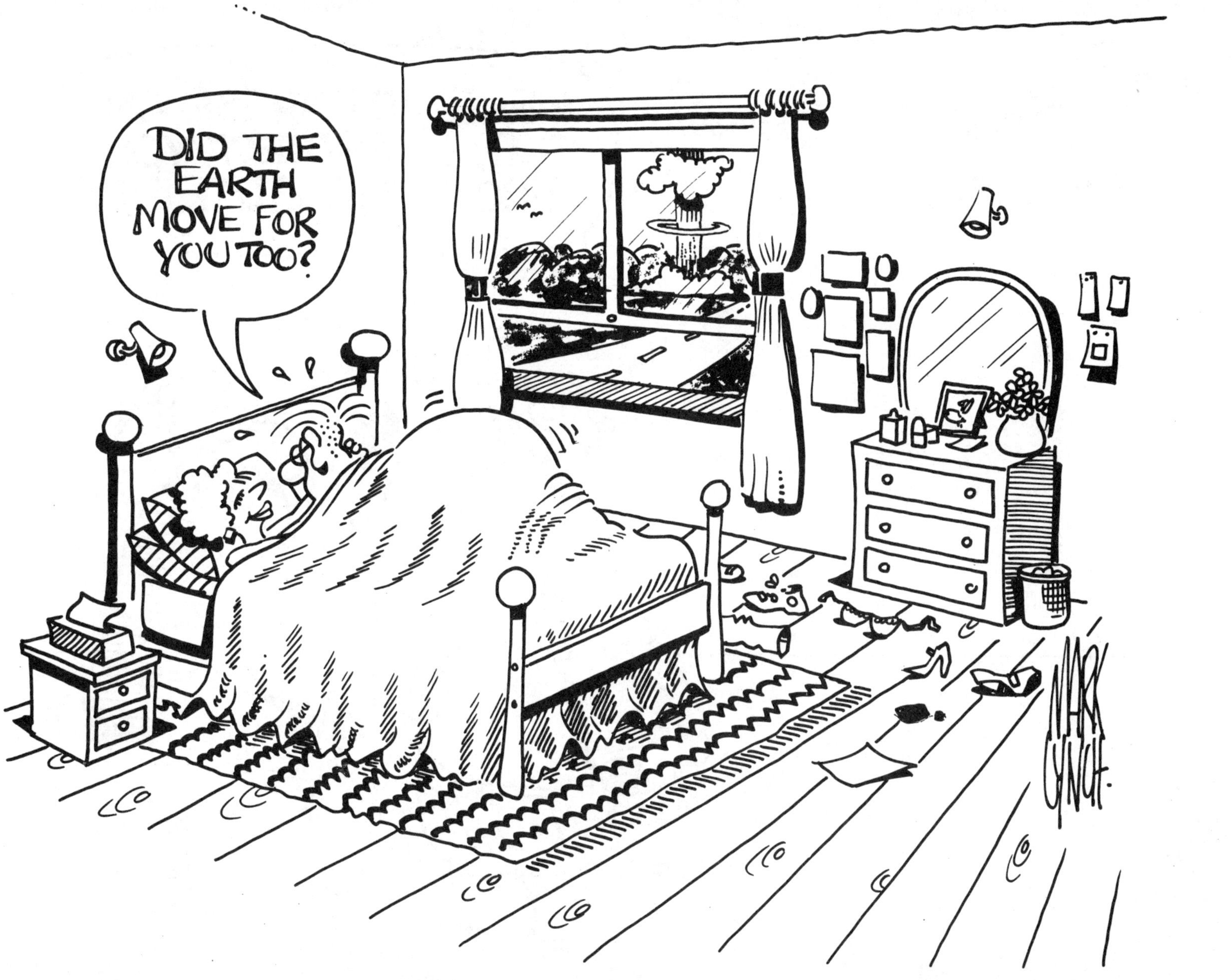
DID THE EARTH MOVE FOR YOU TOO?
MARK LYNCH.

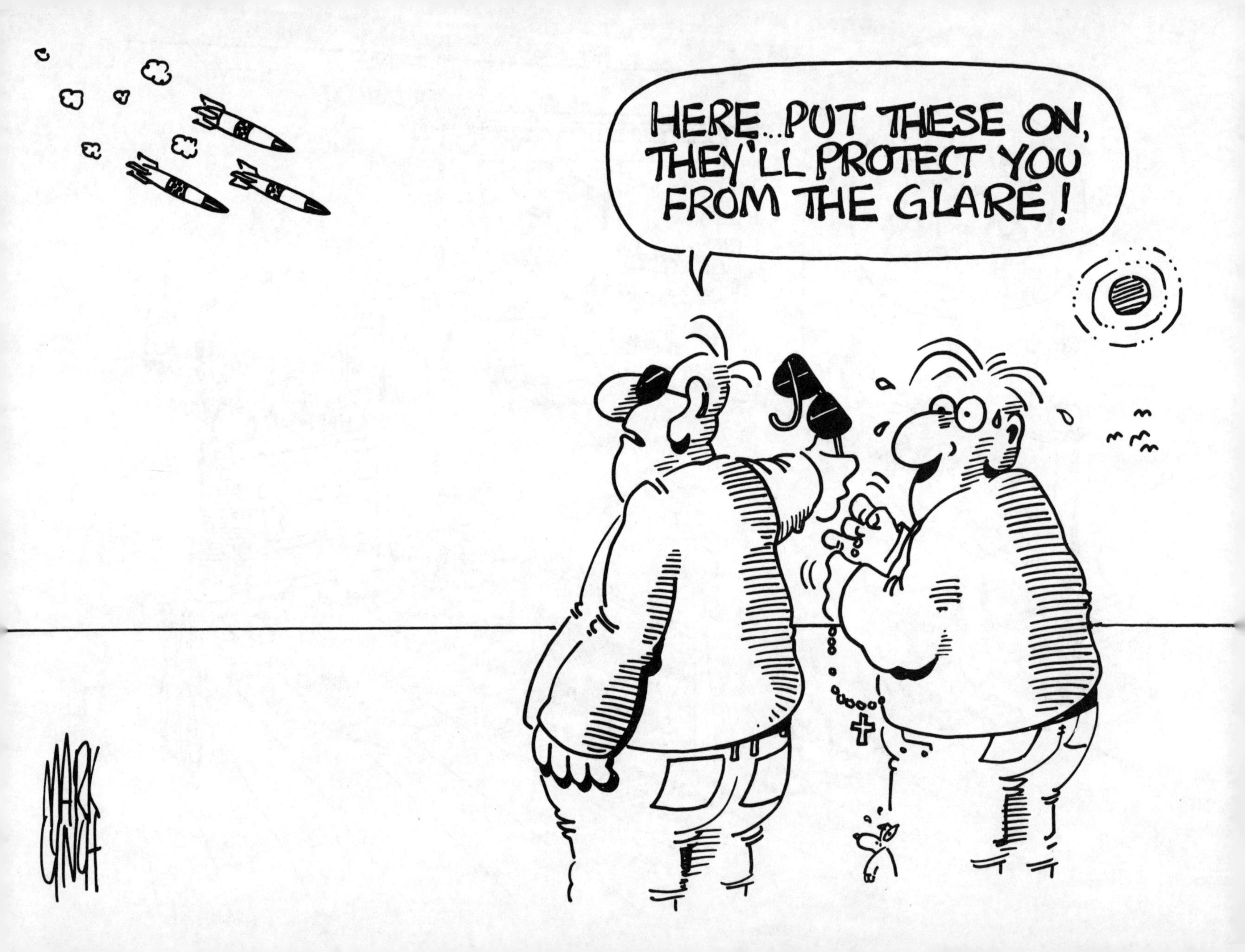
HERE...PUT THESE ON, THEY'LL PROTECT YOU FROM THE GLARE!
MARK LYNCH

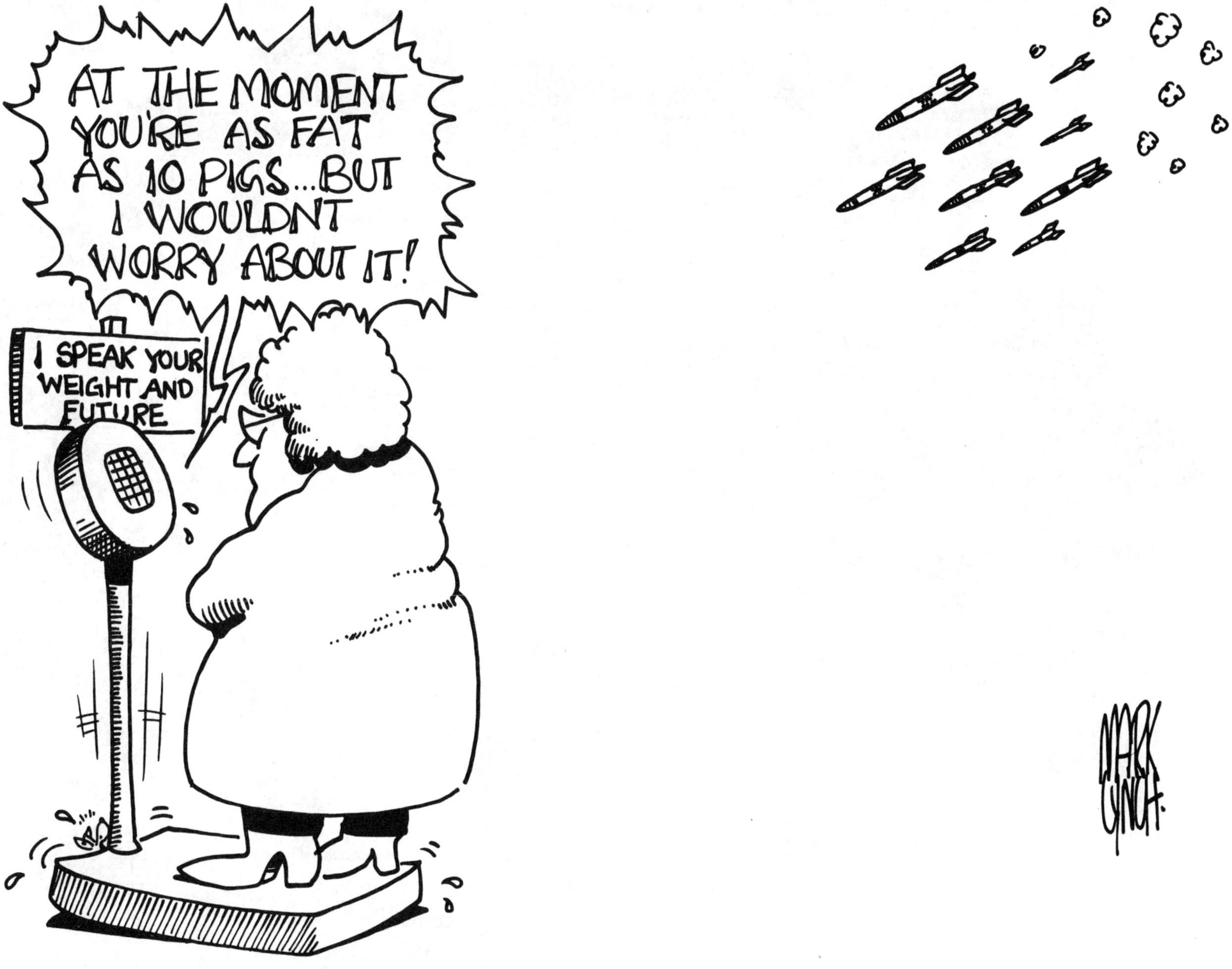
AT THE MOMENT YOU'RE AS FAT AS 10 PIGS...BUT I WOULDNT WORRY ABOUT IT!
I SPEAK YOUR WEIGHT AND FUTURE
MARK LYNCH

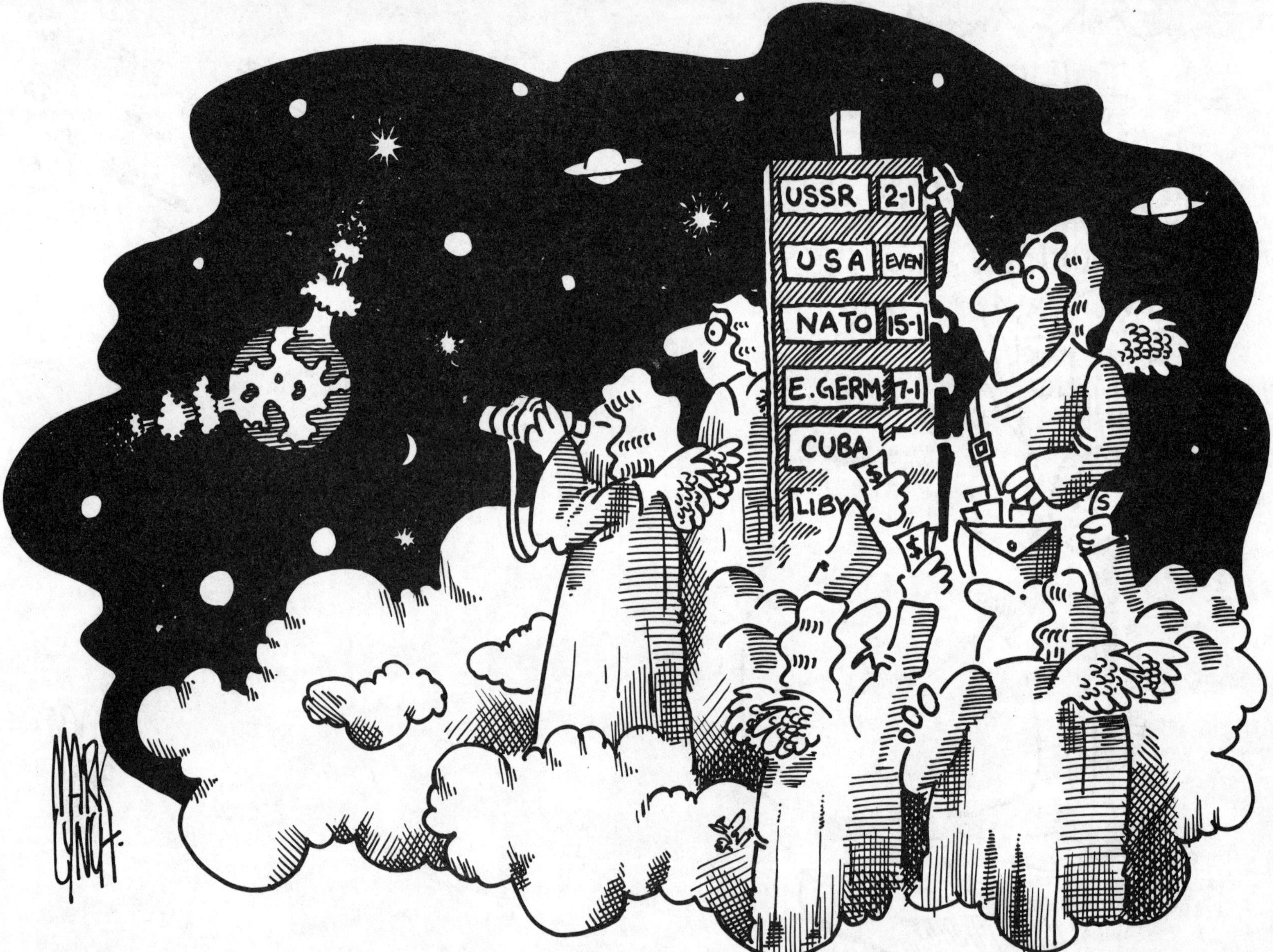
USSR 2-1
USA EVEN
NATO 15-1
E.GERM 7-1
CUBA
LIBY
MARK LYNCH

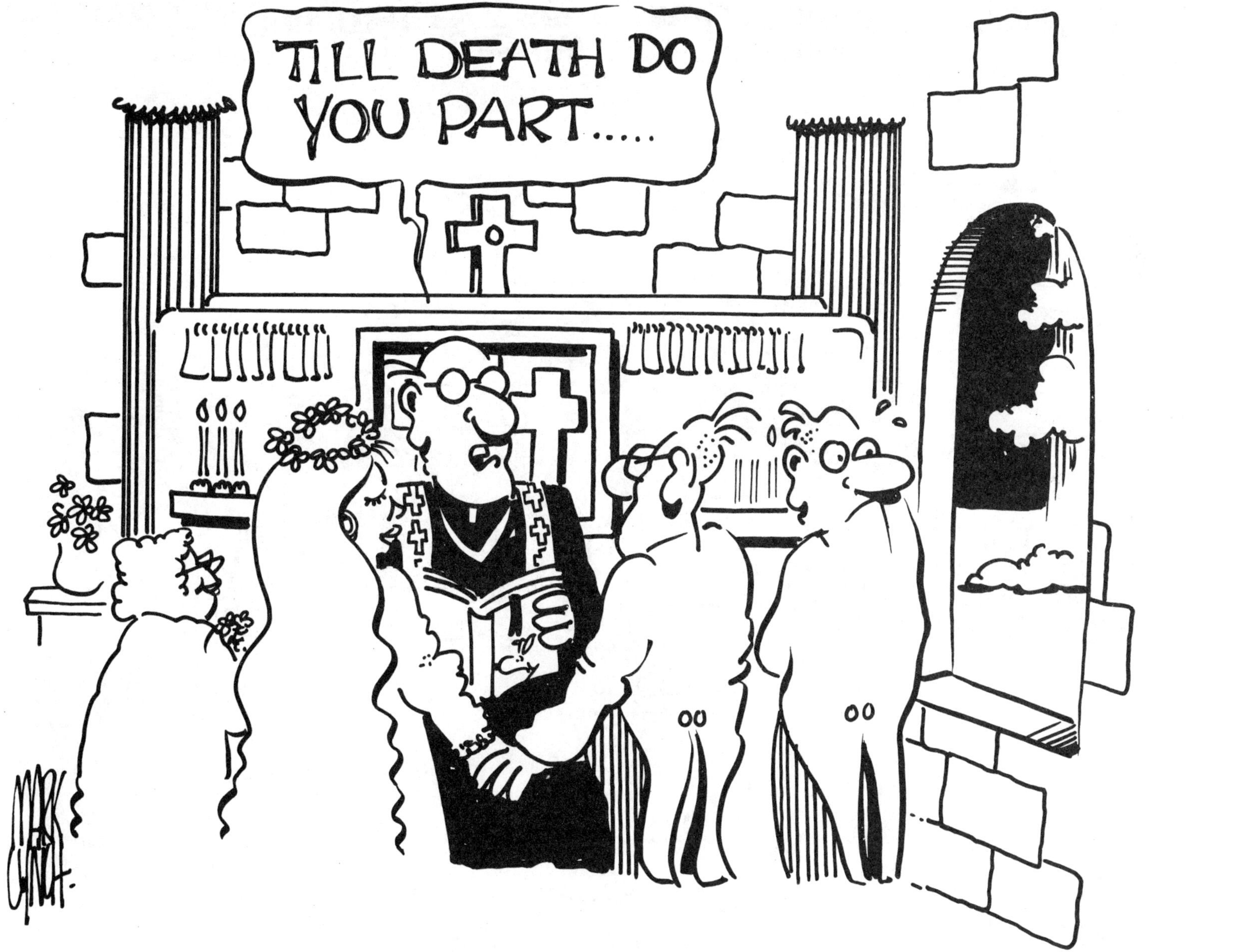
TILL DEATH DO YOU PART.....

COULD NOTHING STOP CARL CAPTURING THE TITLE THAT HAD ELUDED HIM FOR SO MANY YEARS?

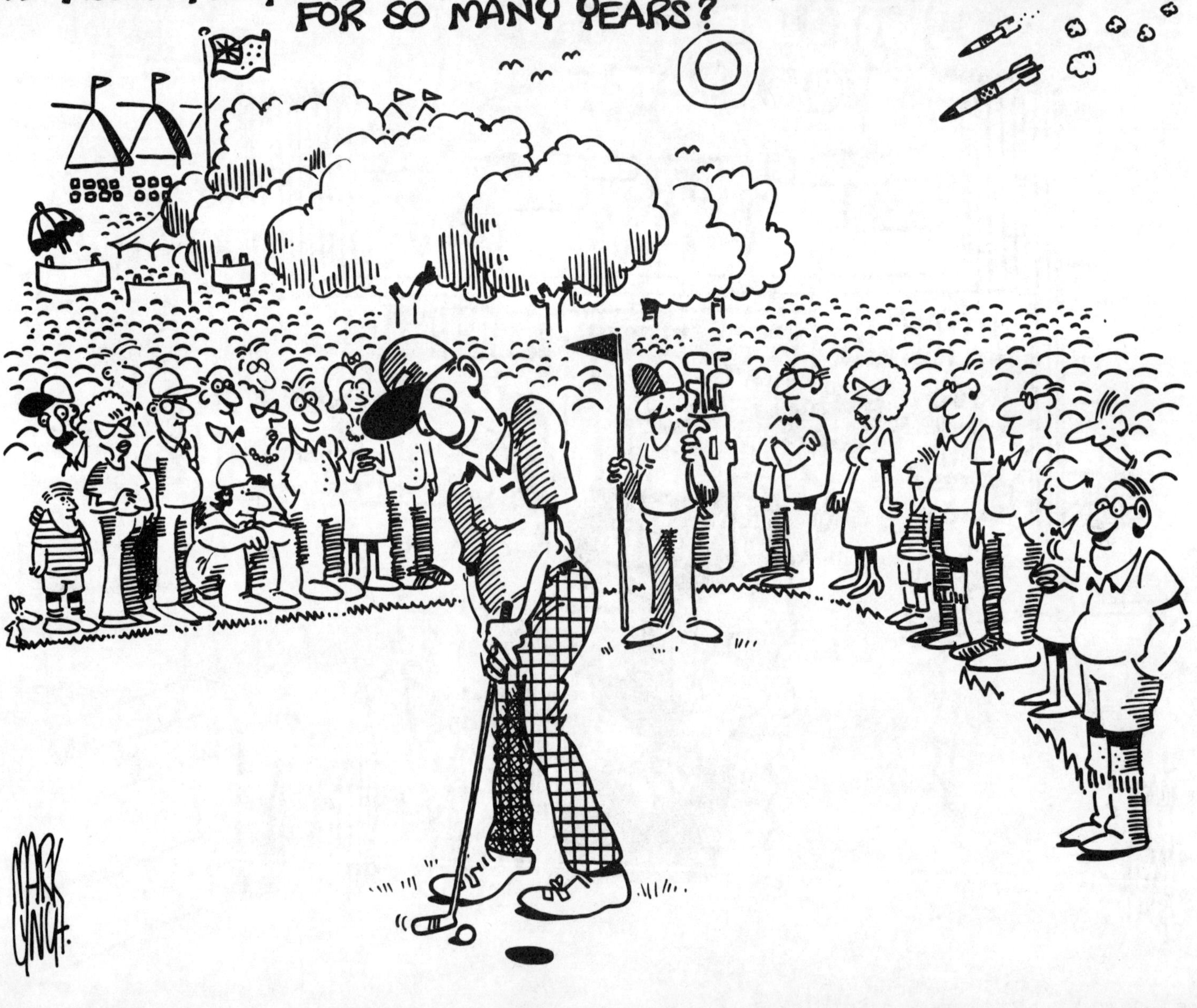

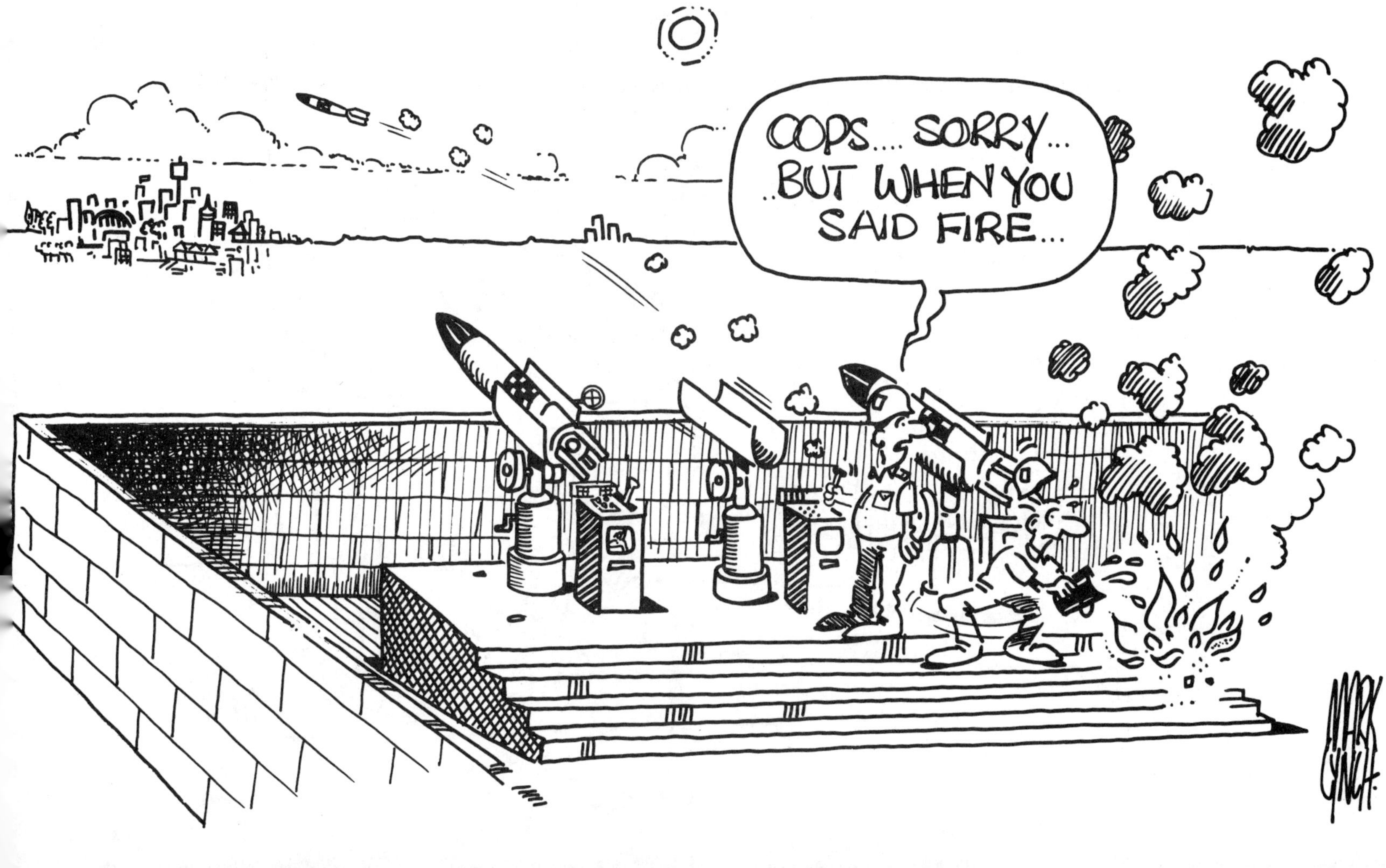
OOPS.... SORRY...
..BUT WHEN YOU
SAID FIRE...
MARK LYNCH.

A GROUP OF HIGH POWERED NEGOTIATORS TRYING TO CONVINCE A NEWCOMER THAT THE WORLD ISN'T SUCH A BAD PLACE TO VISIT!

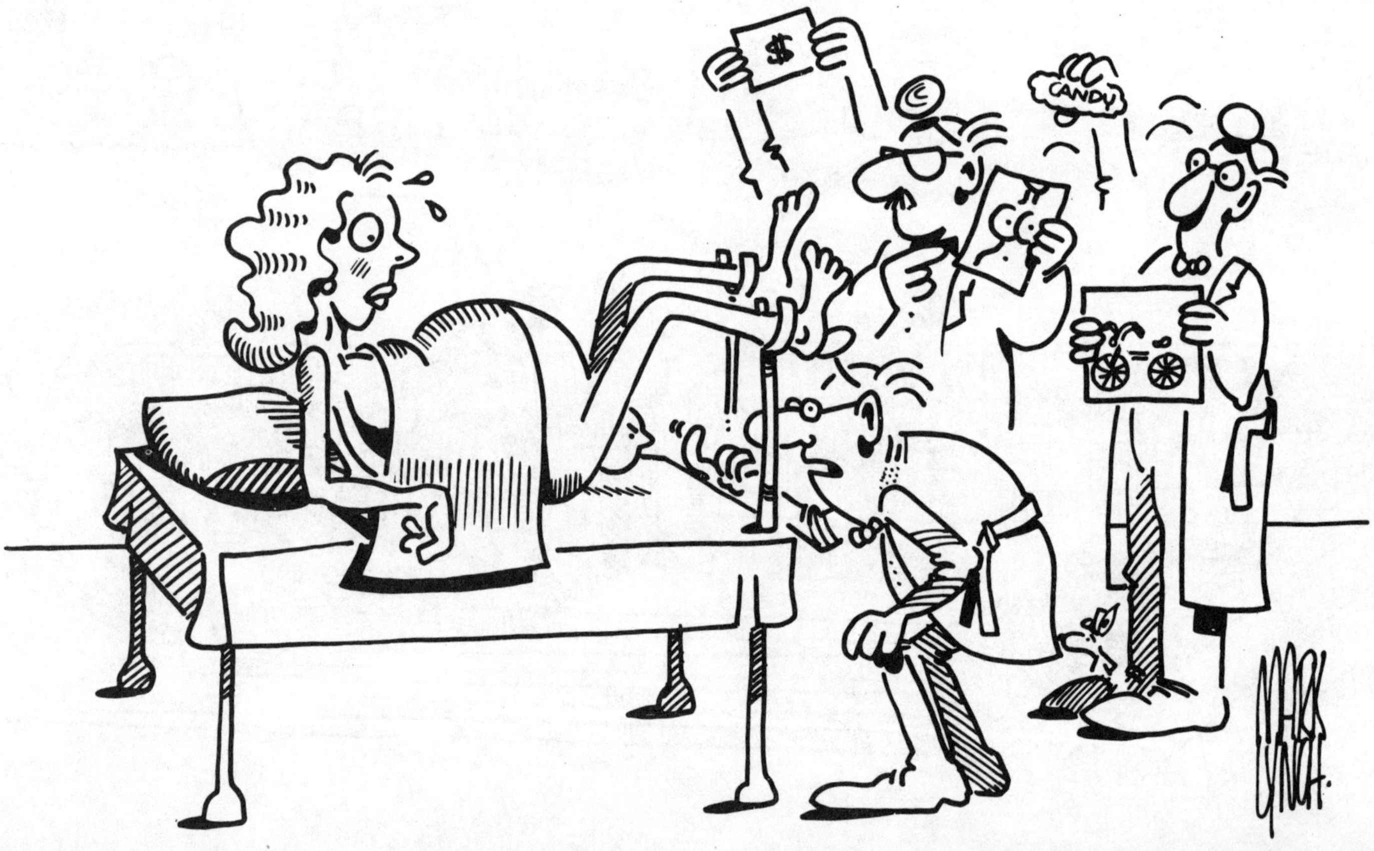
$
CANDY

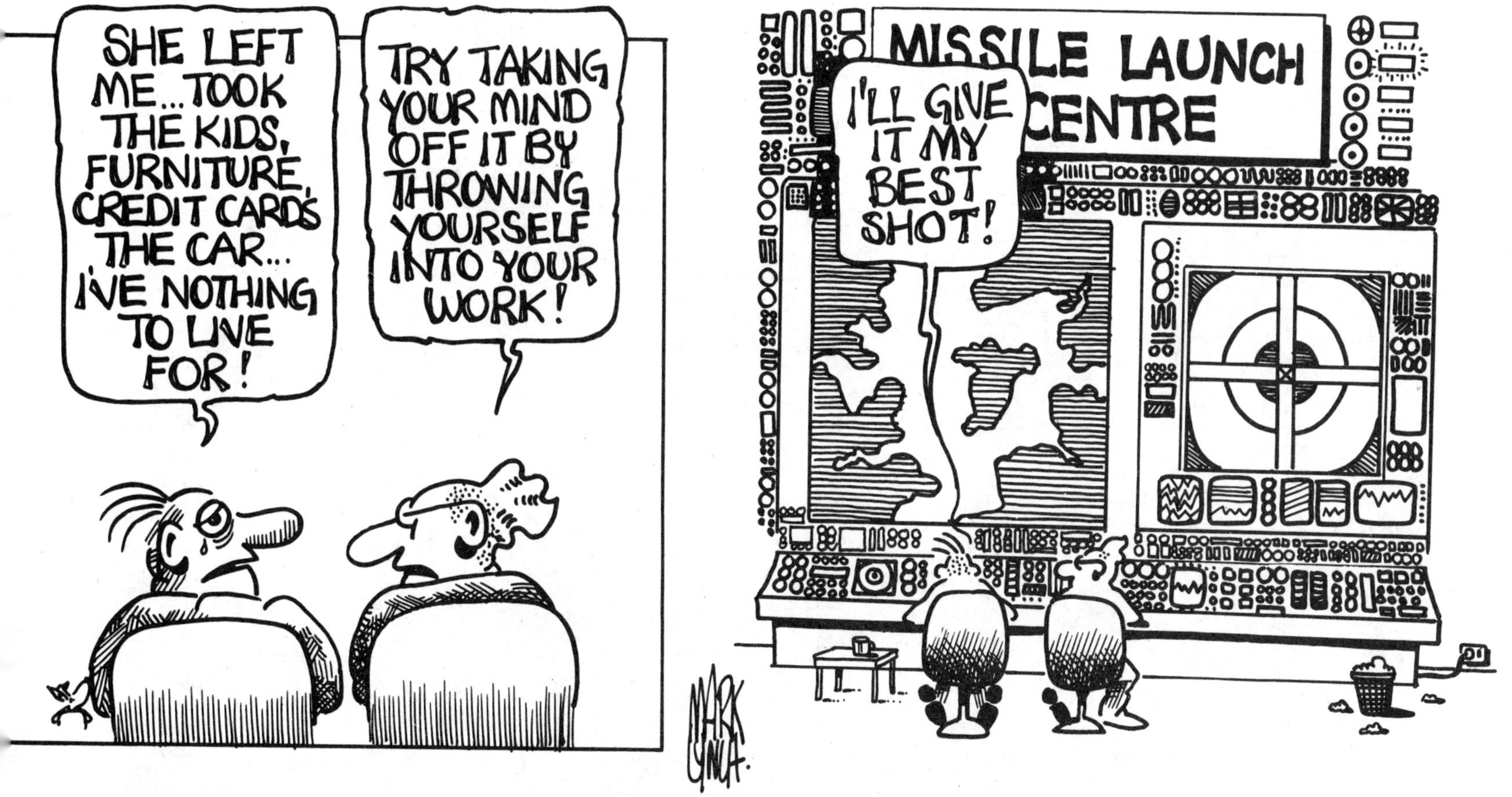
SHE LEFT ME... TOOK THE KIDS, FURNITURE, CREDIT CARDS THE CAR... I'VE NOTHING TO LIVE FOR!
TRY TAKING YOUR MIND OFF IT BY THROWING YOURSELF INTO YOUR WORK!
MISSILE LAUNCH CENTRE
I'LL GIVE IT MY BEST SHOT!

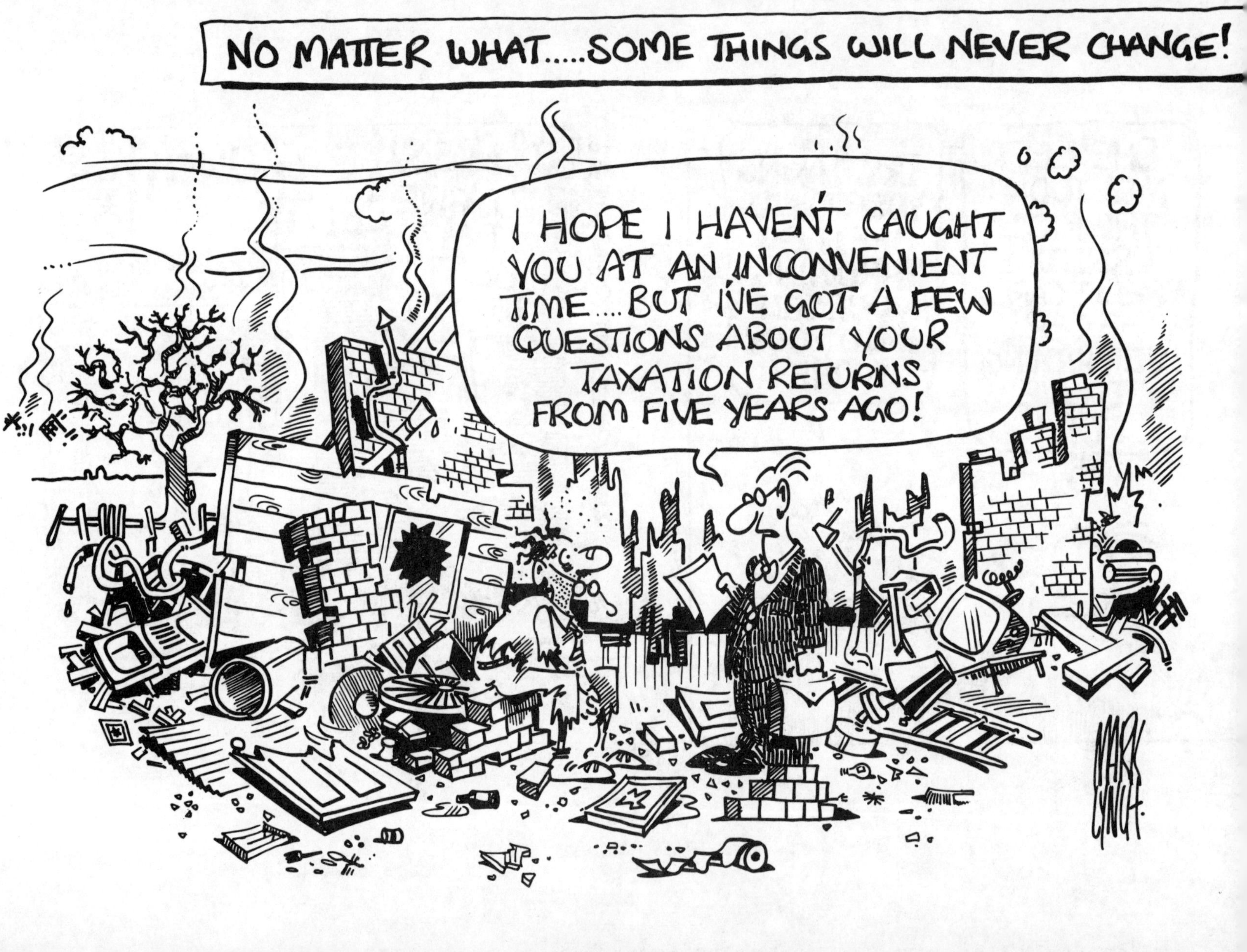
NO MATTER WHAT.....SOME THINGS WILL NEVER CHANGE!
I HOPE I HAVEN'T CAUGHT YOU AT AN INCONVENIENT TIME.....BUT I'VE GOT A FEW QUESTIONS ABOUT YOUR TAXATION RETURNS FROM FIVE YEARS AGO!
MARK LYNCH.

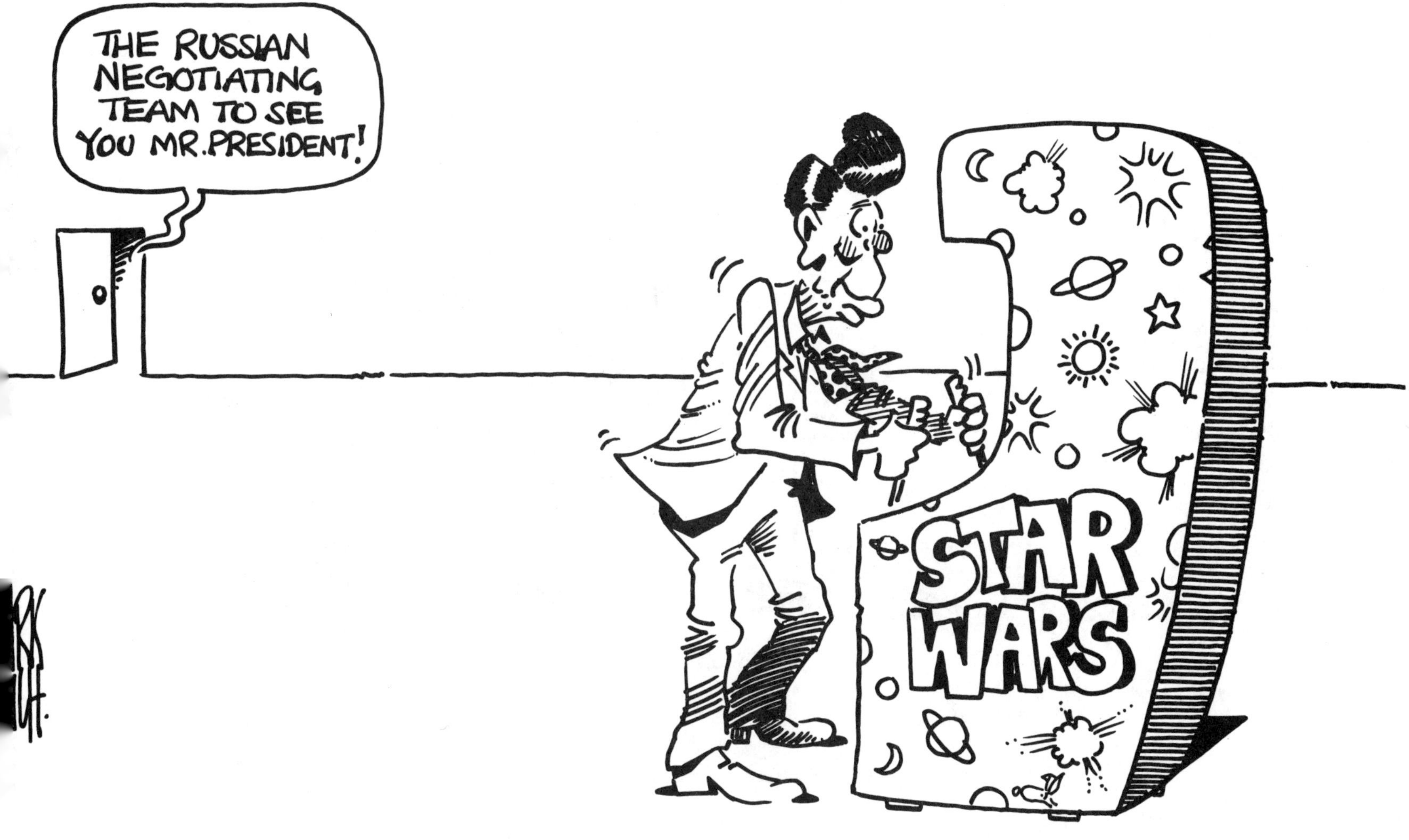
THE RUSSIAN NEGOTIATING TEAM TO SEE YOU MR. PRESIDENT!
STAR WARS

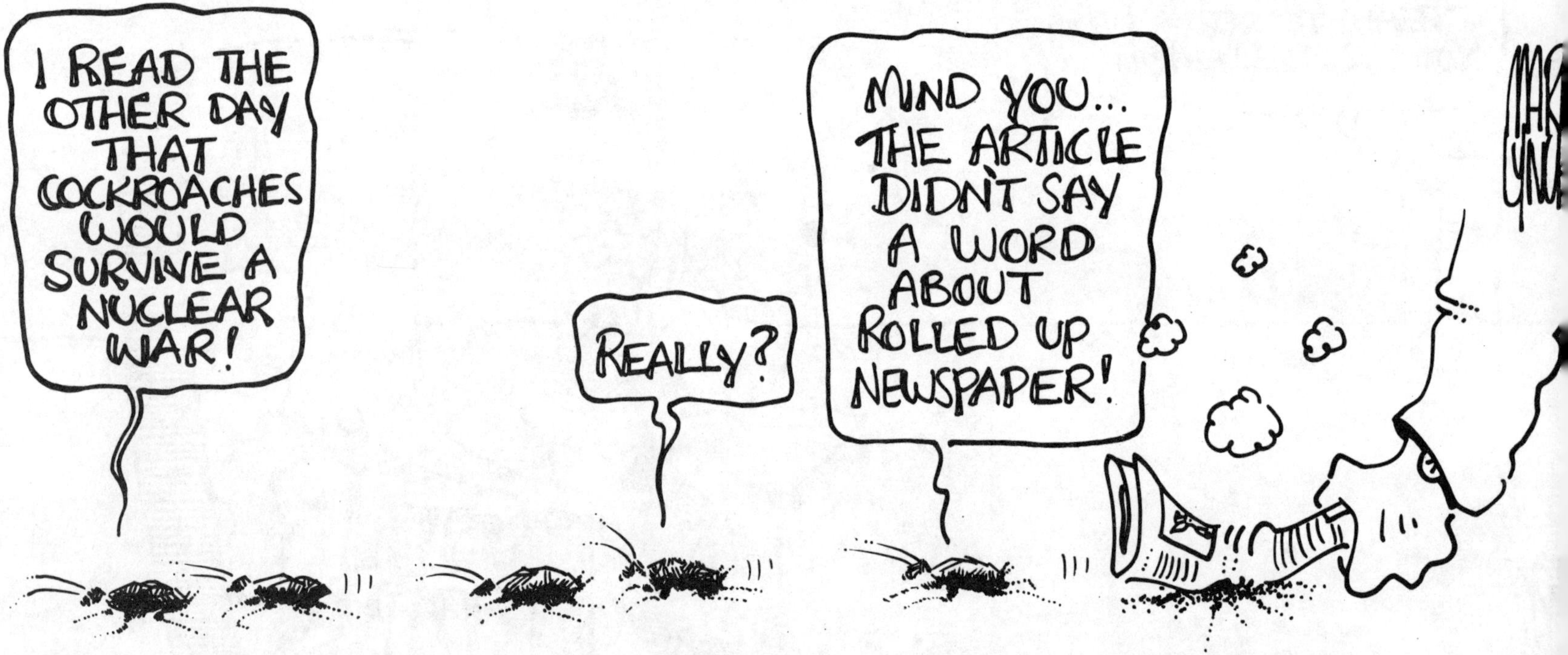
I READ THE OTHER DAY THAT COCKROACHES WOULD SURVIVE A NUCLEAR WAR!
REALLY?
MIND YOU... THE ARTICLE DIDN'T SAY A WORD ABOUT ROLLED UP NEWSPAPER!

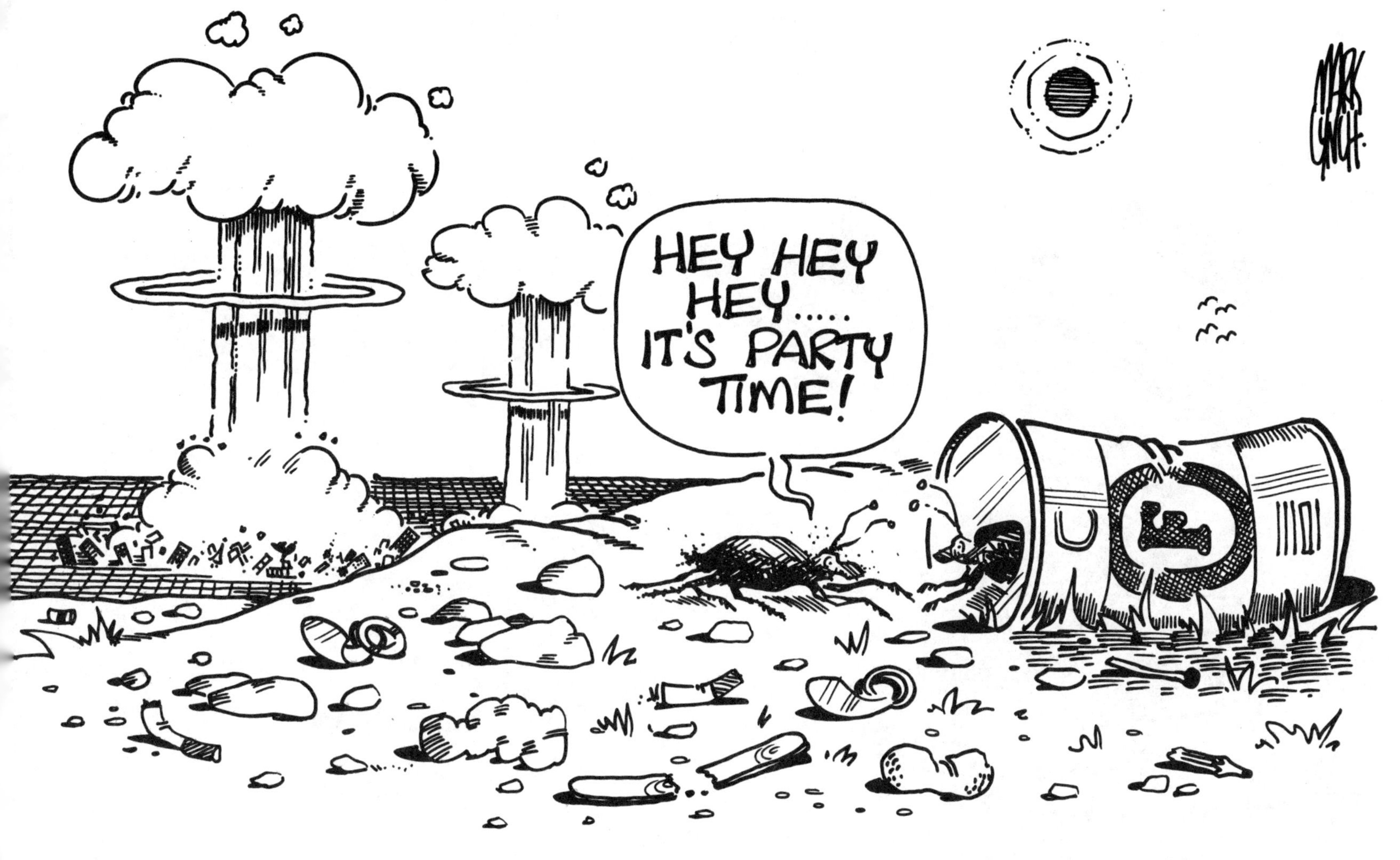
HEY HEY HEY..... IT'S PARTY TIME!

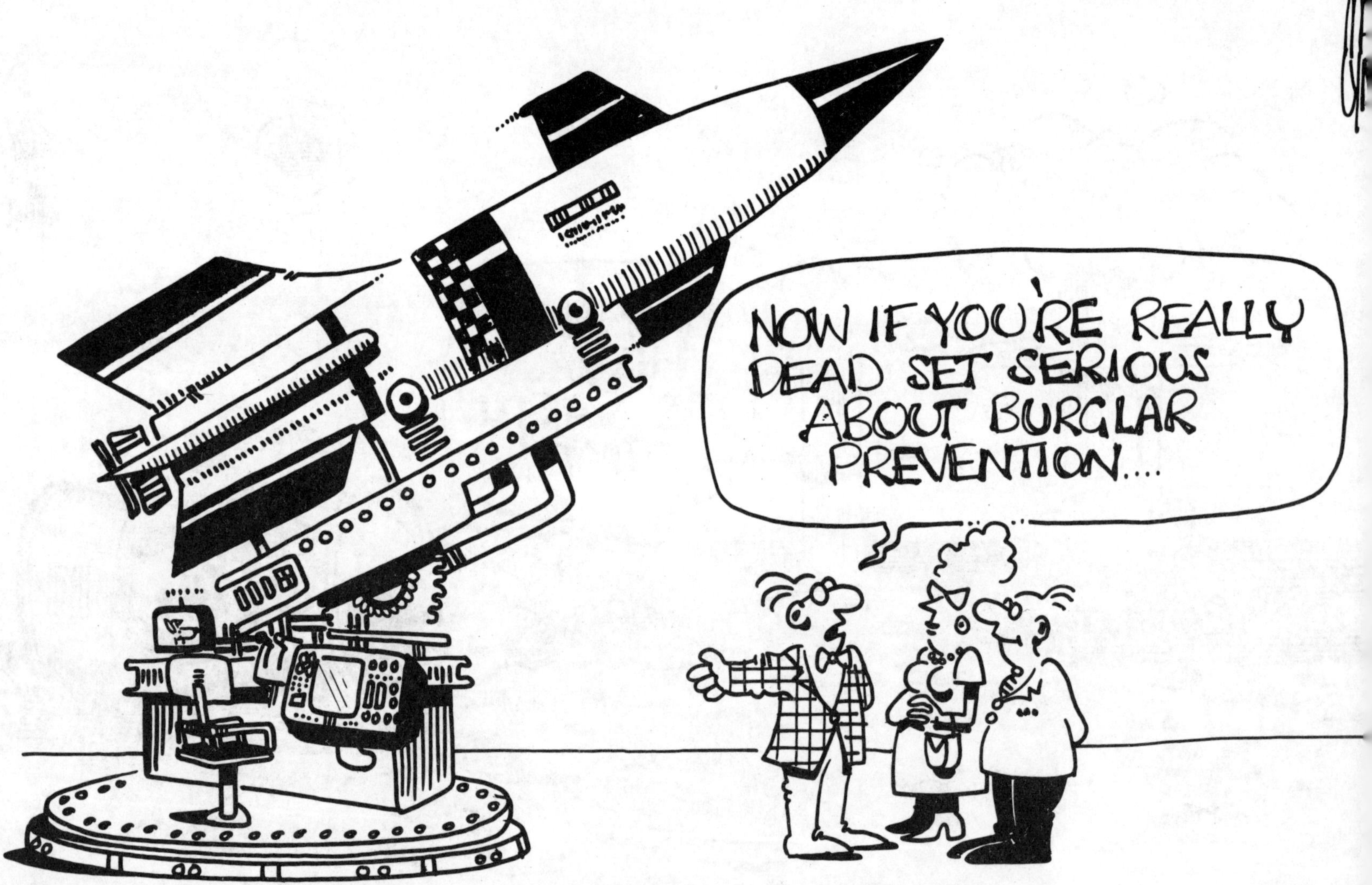
NOW IF YOU'RE REALLY DEAD SET SERIOUS ABOUT BURGLAR PREVENTION....

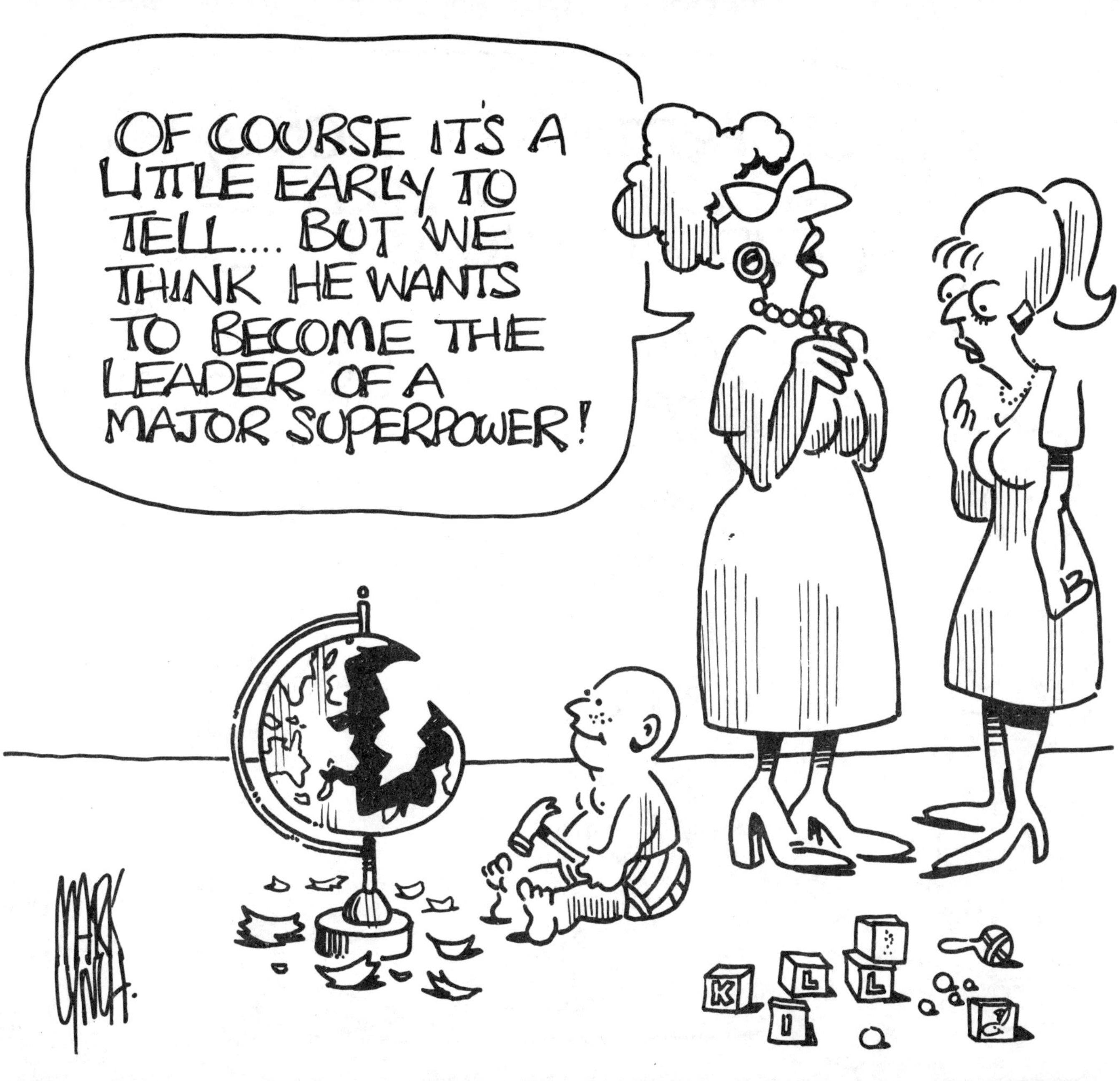
OF COURSE IT'S A LITTLE EARLY TO TELL.... BUT WE THINK HE WANTS TO BECOME THE LEADER OF A MAJOR SUPERPOWER!

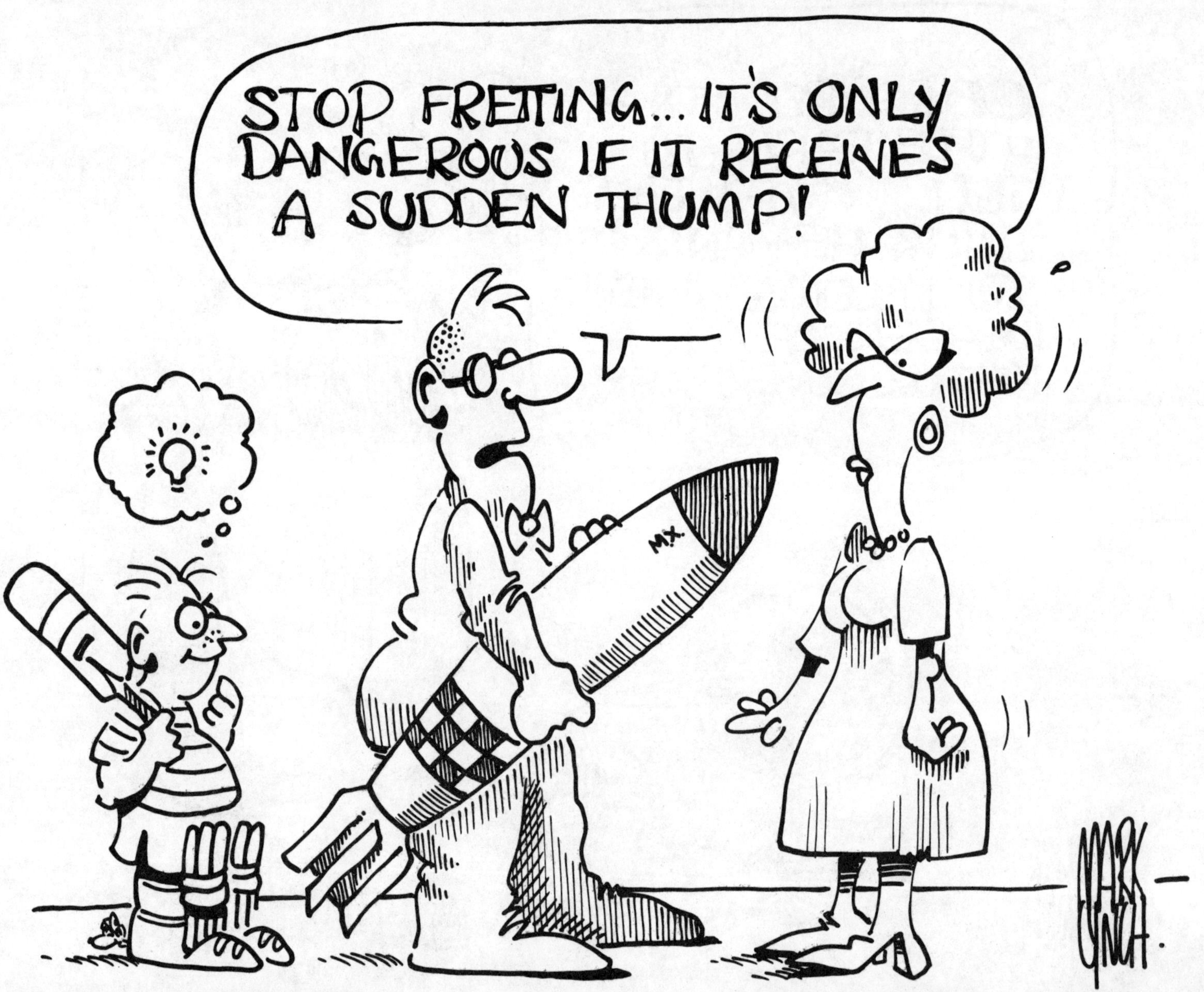
STOP FRETTING... IT'S ONLY DANGEROUS IF IT RECEIVES A SUDDEN THUMP!
M.X.

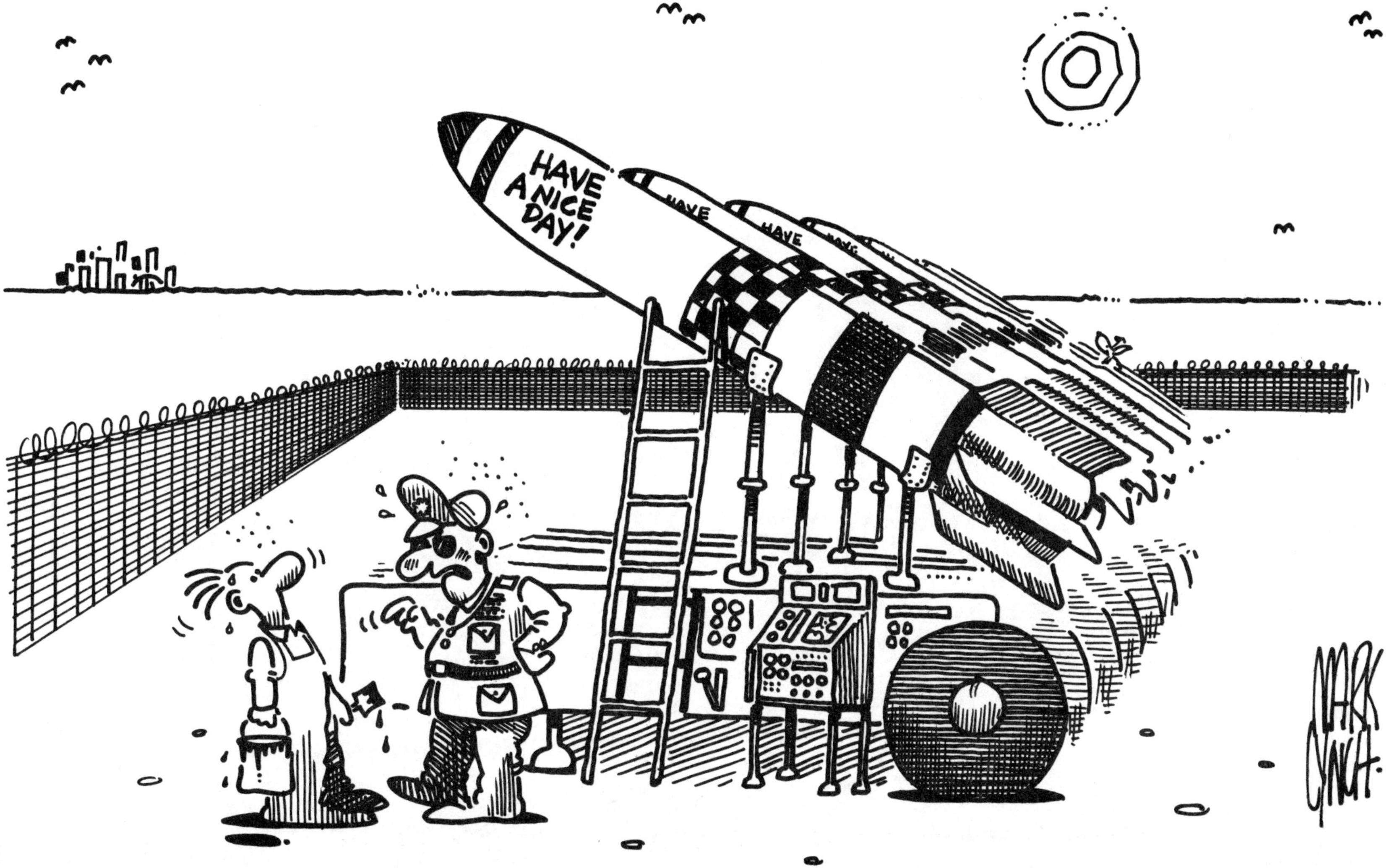
HAVE A NICE DAY!
HAVE
HAVE

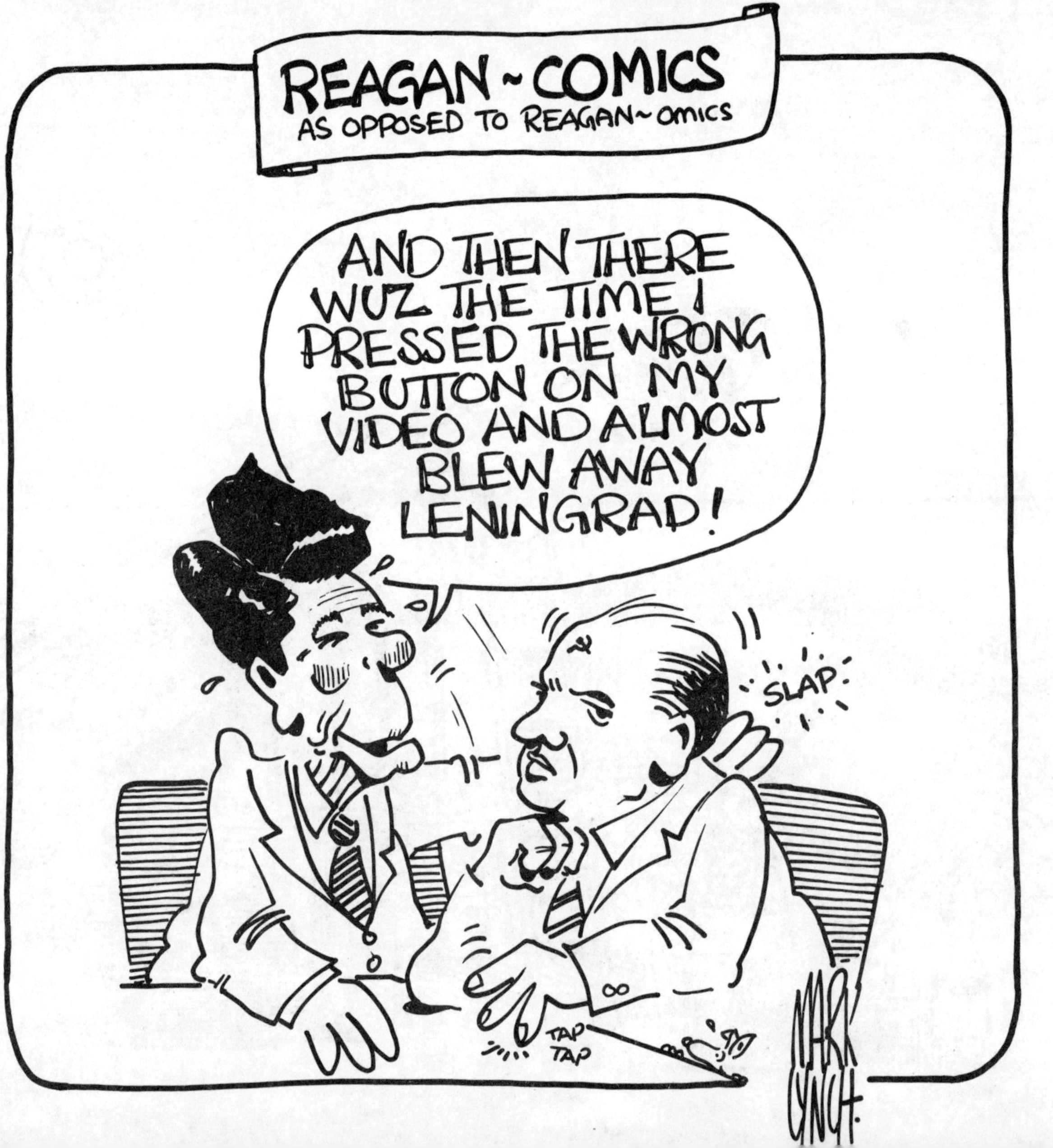
REAGAN ~ COMICS
AS OPPOSED TO REAGAN ~ OMICS
AND THEN THERE WUZ THE TIME I PRESSED THE WRONG BUTTON ON MY VIDEO AND ALMOST BLEW AWAY LENINGRAD!
SLAP
TAP TAP
MARK LYNCH

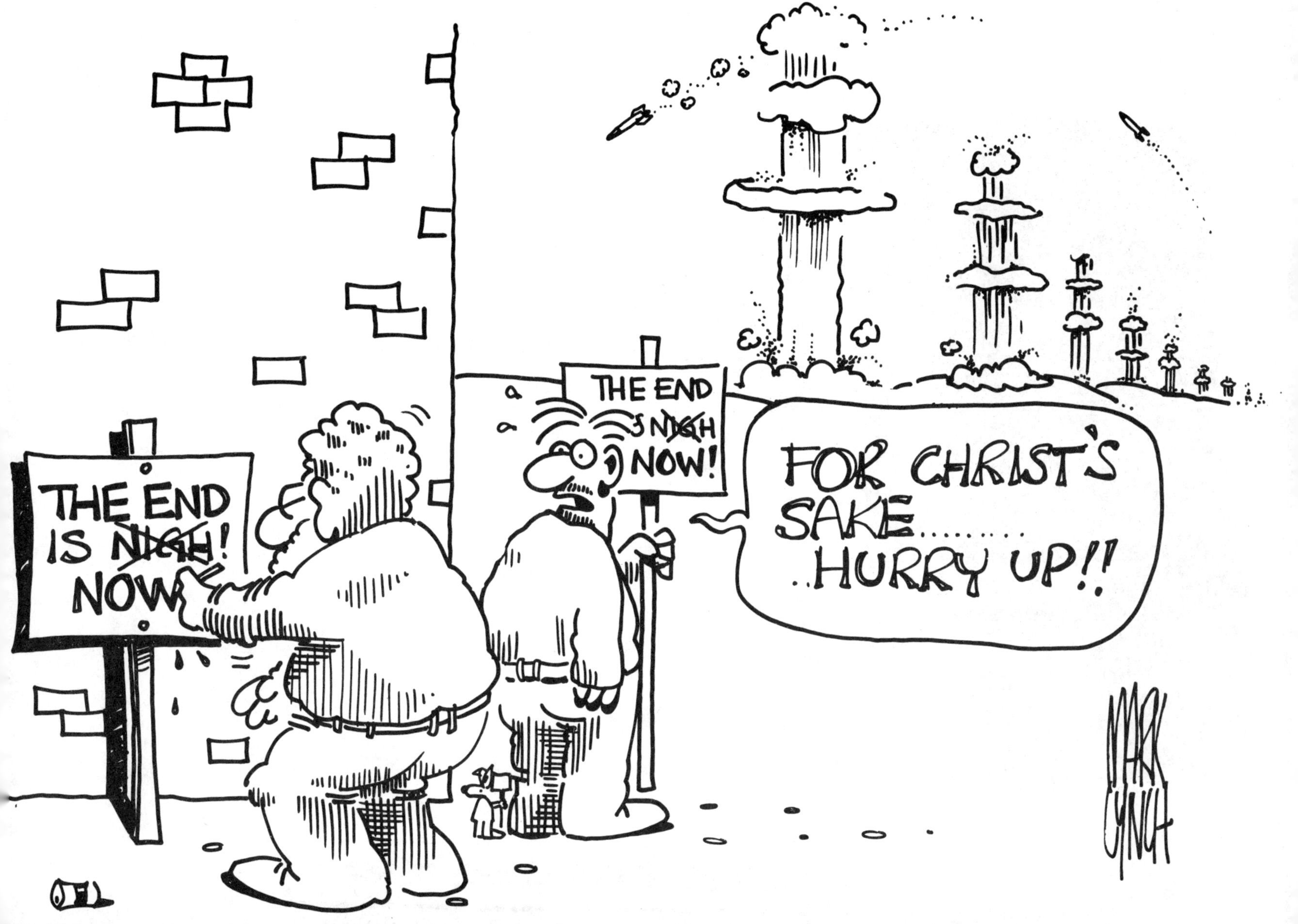
THE END IS ~~NIGH~~! NOW
THE END
S ~~NIGH~~
NOW!
FOR CHRIST'S SAKE.........
..HURRY UP!!
MARK LYNCH

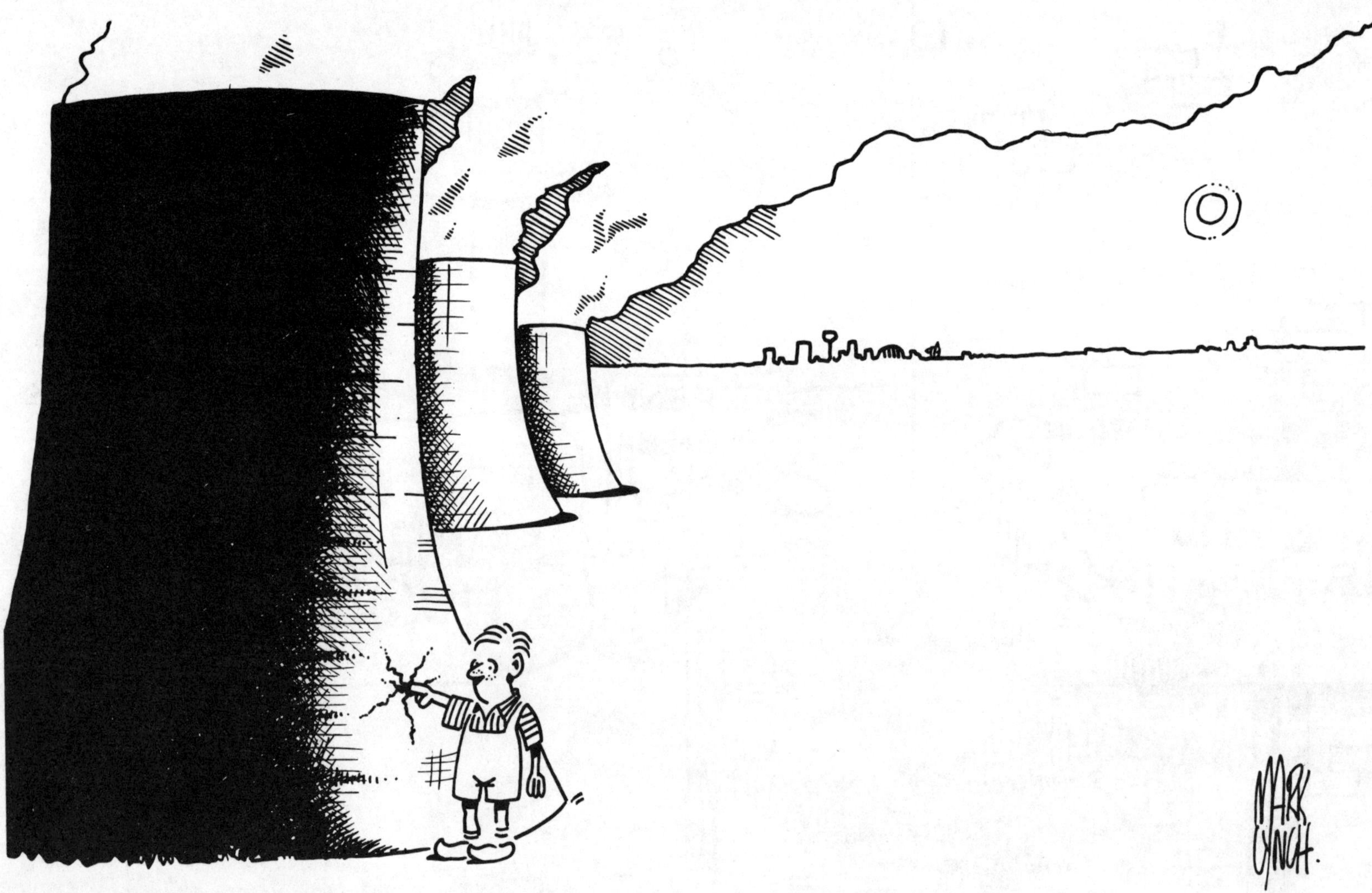
MARK LYNCH.

THESE CHANGING TIMES.

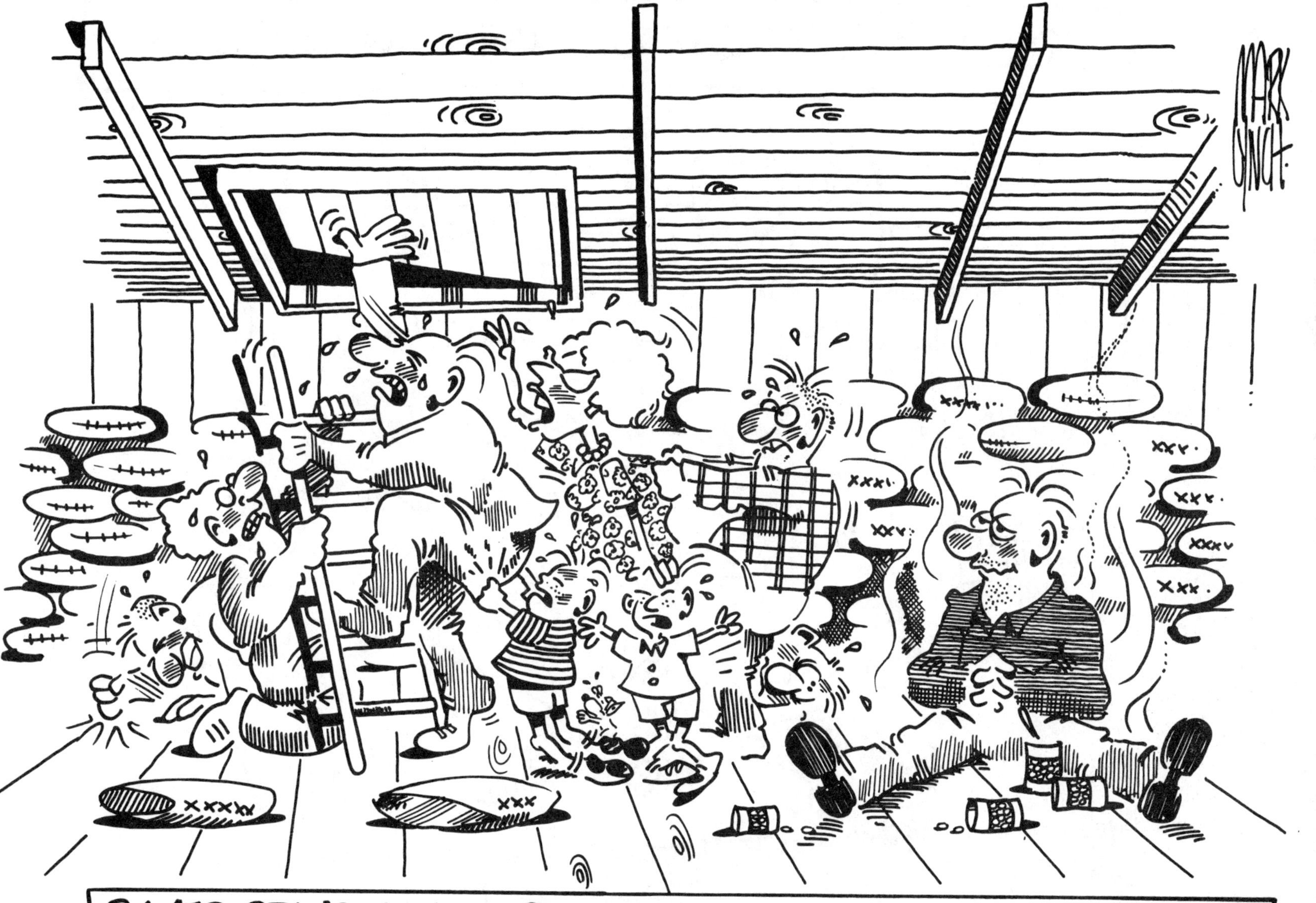

BAKED BEANS MAY NOT BE THE BEST FOOD FOR FALLOUT SHELTERS!

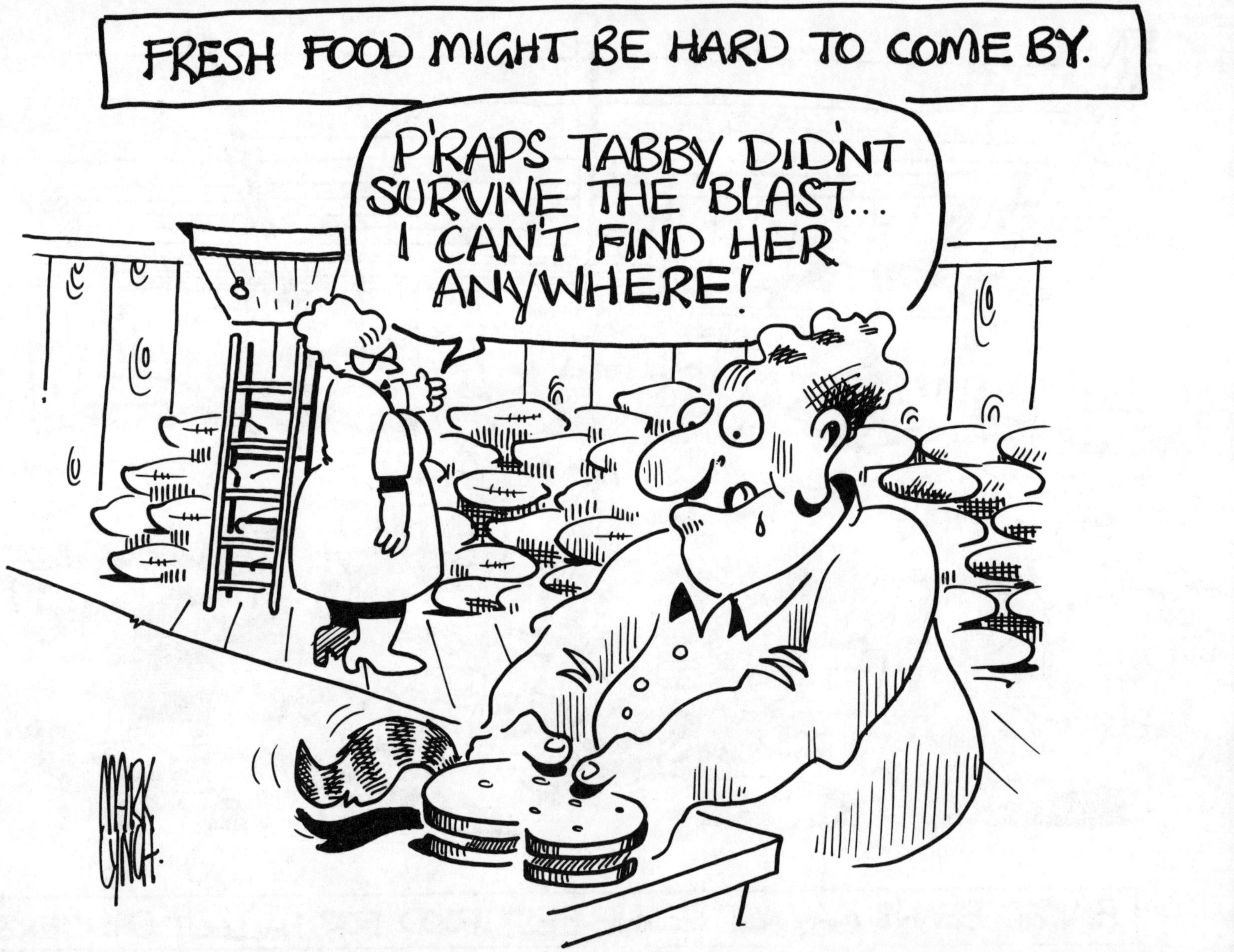
FRESH FOOD MIGHT BE HARD TO COME BY.
P'RAPS TABBY DIDN'T SURVIVE THE BLAST... I CAN'T FIND HER ANYWHERE!
MARK LYNCH.

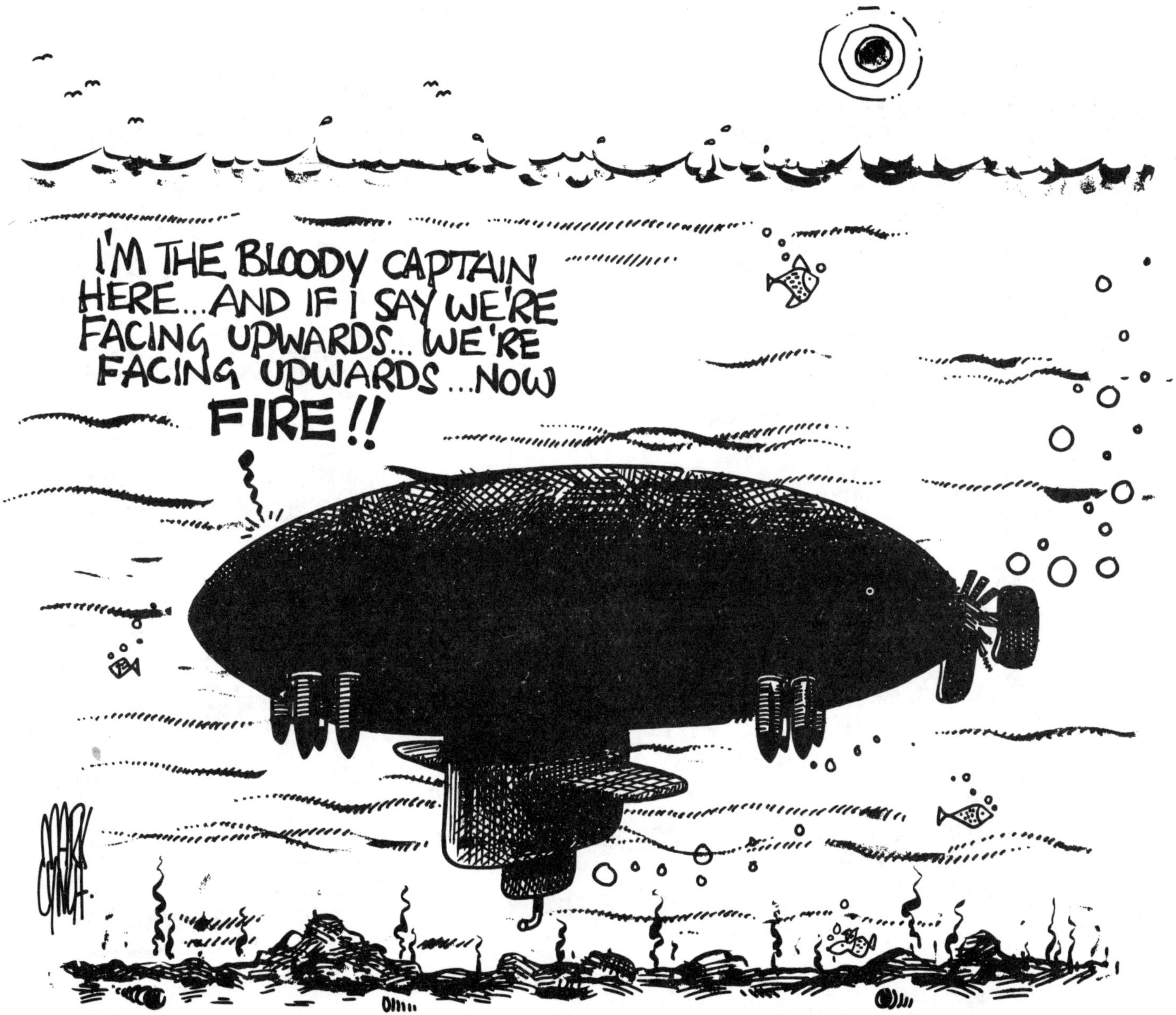
I'M THE BLOODY CAPTAIN HERE...AND IF I SAY WE'RE FACING UPWARDS... WE'RE FACING UPWARDS...NOW FIRE!!

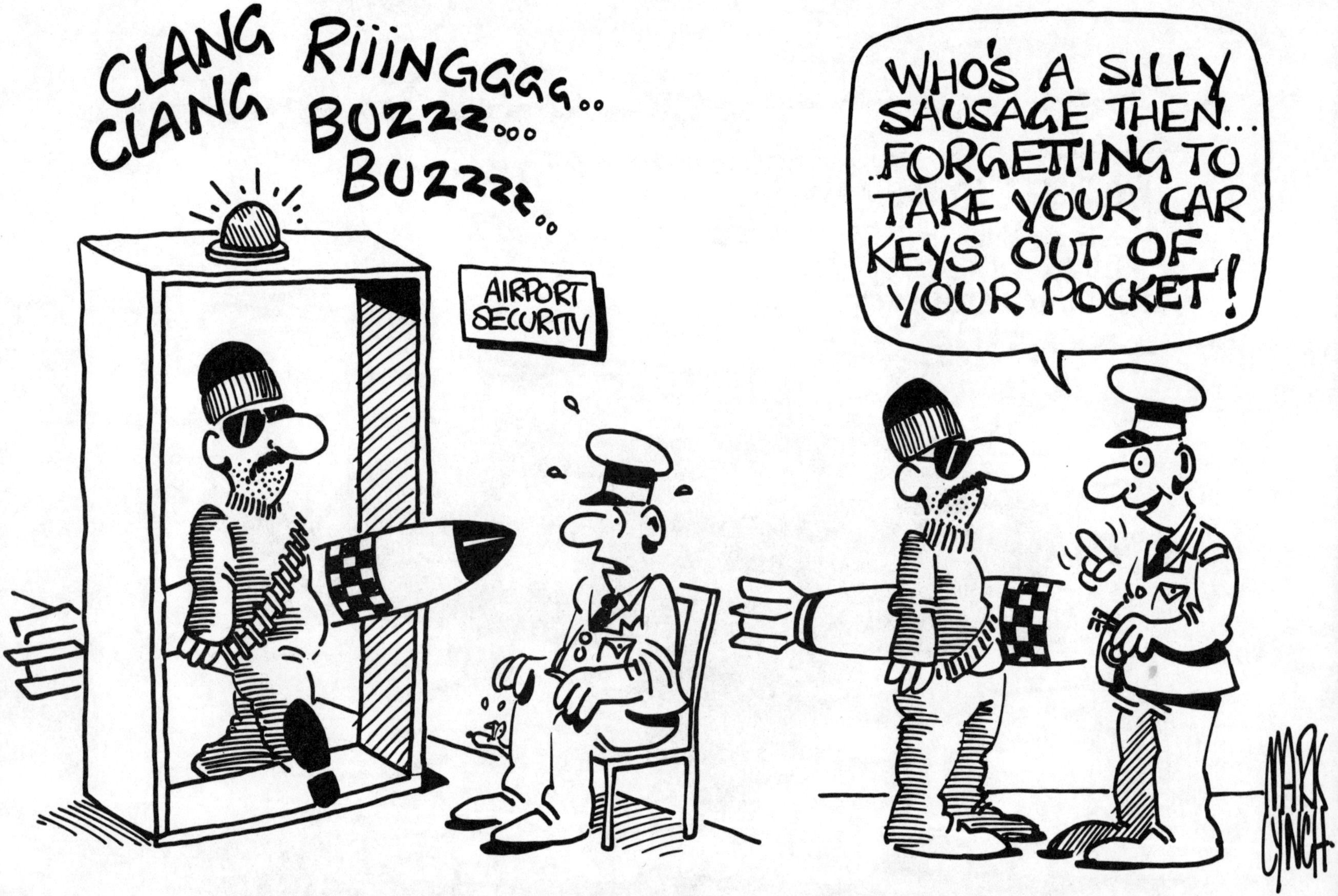
CLANG CLANG
RIIINGGGG.. BUZZZ... BUZZZZZ..
AIRPORT SECURITY
WHO'S A SILLY SAUSAGE THEN... FORGETTING TO TAKE YOUR CAR KEYS OUT OF YOUR POCKET!
MARK LYNCH

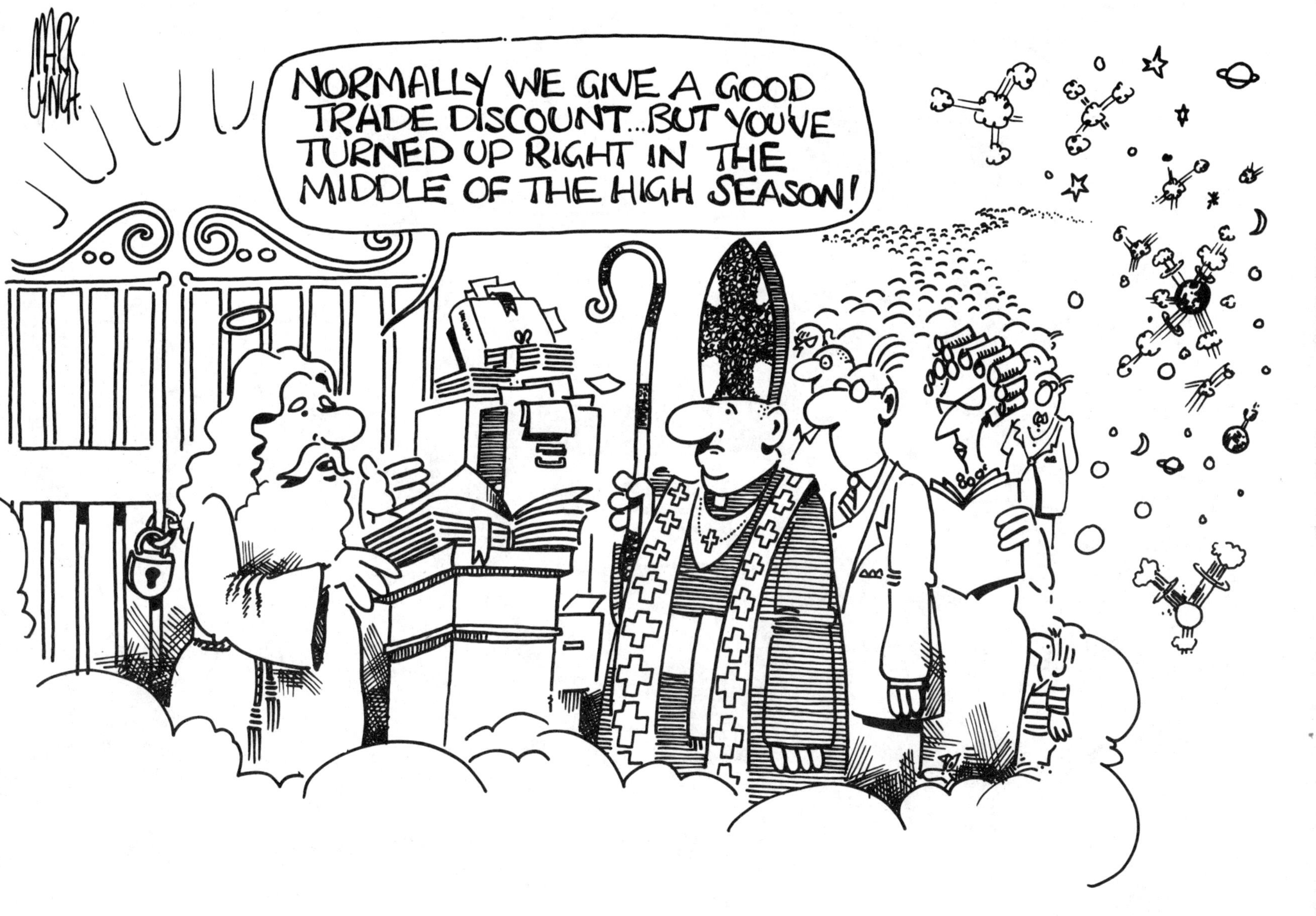
NORMALLY WE GIVE A GOOD TRADE DISCOUNT...BUT YOU'VE TURNED UP RIGHT IN THE MIDDLE OF THE HIGH SEASON!
MARK LYNCH

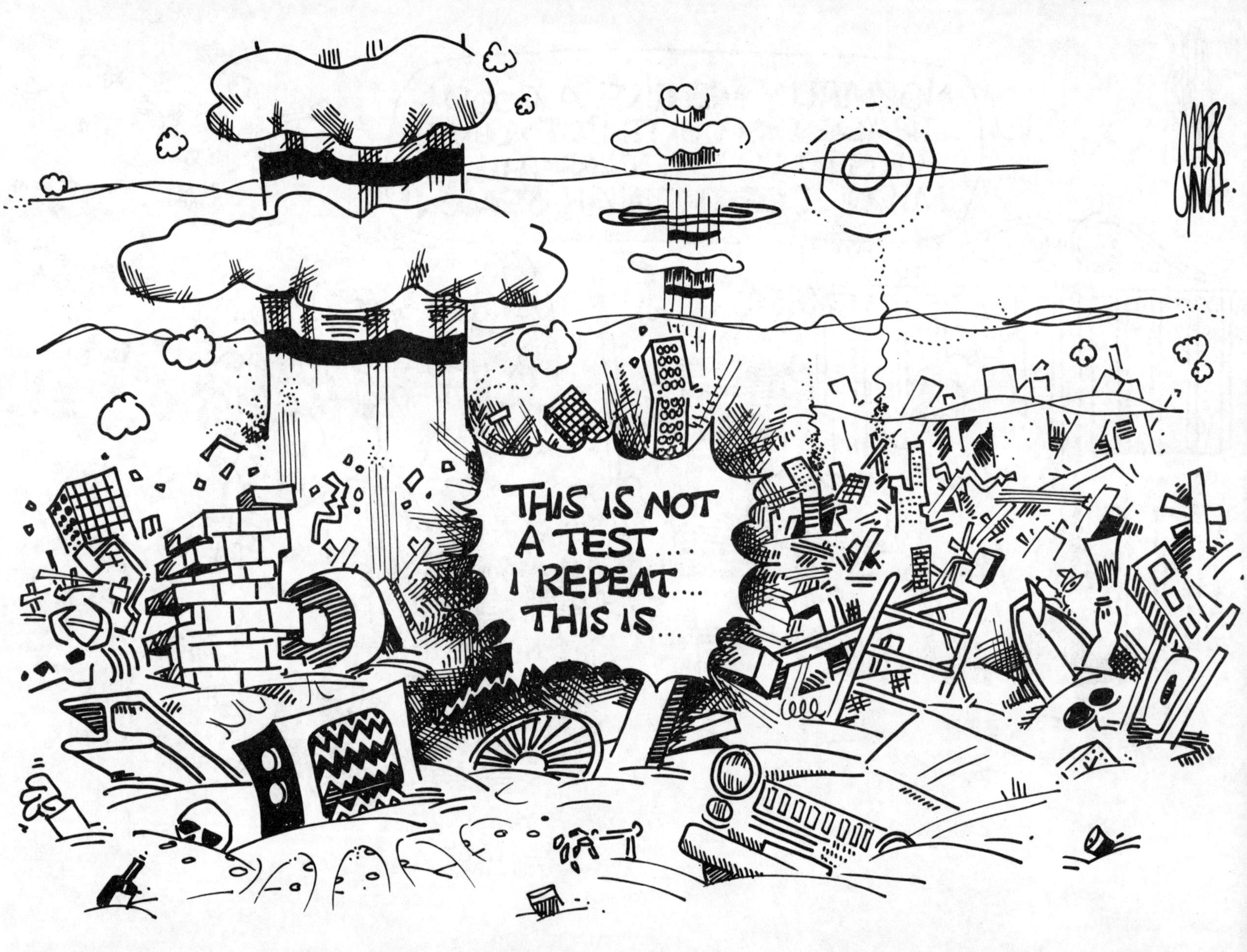
THIS IS NOT
A TEST....
I REPEAT....
THIS IS...

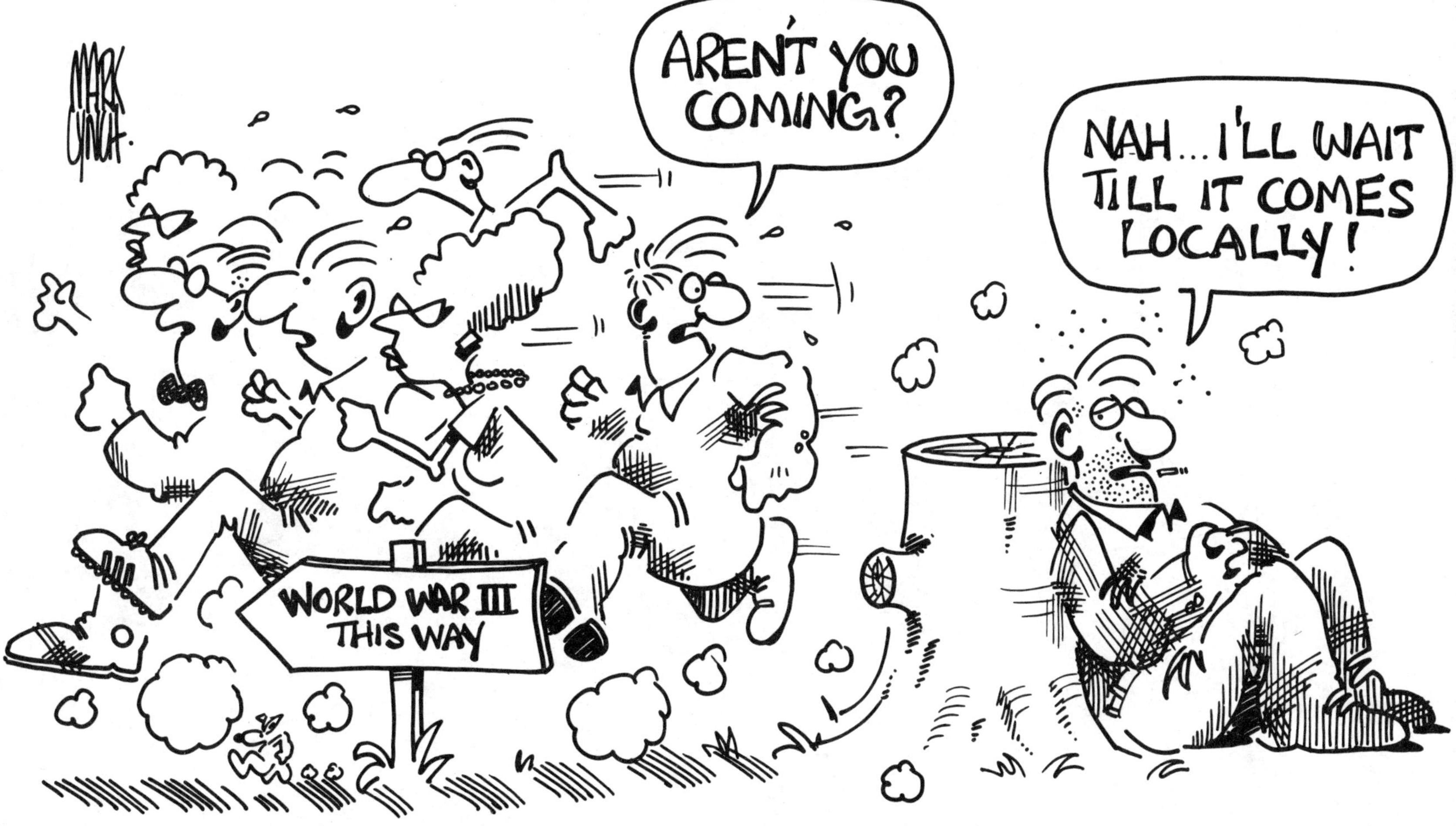
MARK LYNCH.
AREN'T YOU COMING?
NAH... I'LL WAIT TILL IT COMES LOCALLY!
WORLD WAR III THIS WAY

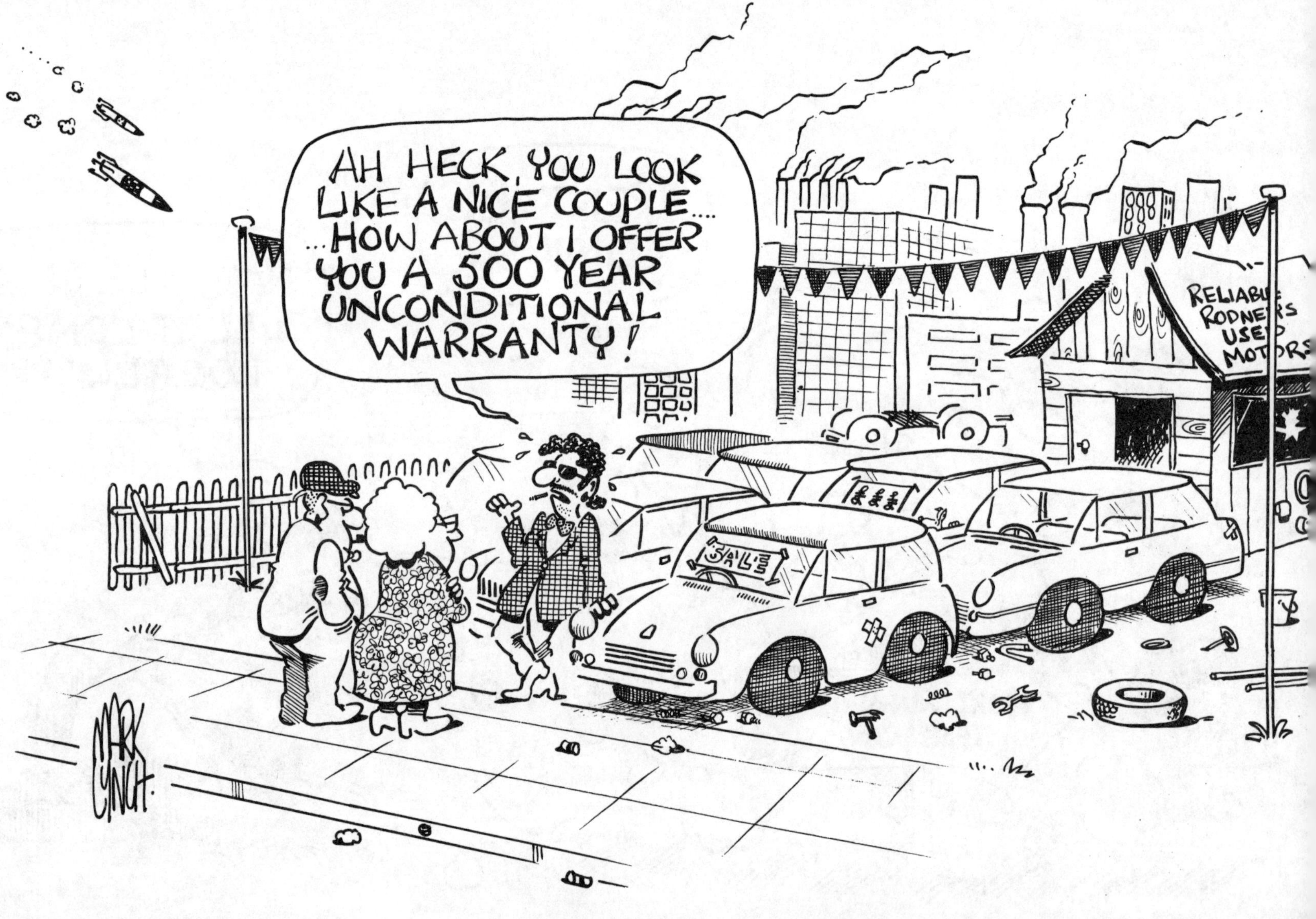
AH HECK, YOU LOOK LIKE A NICE COUPLE.... ...HOW ABOUT I OFFER YOU A 500 YEAR UNCONDITIONAL WARRANTY!
RELIABLE RODNEY'S USED MOTORS
SALE
MARK LYNCH

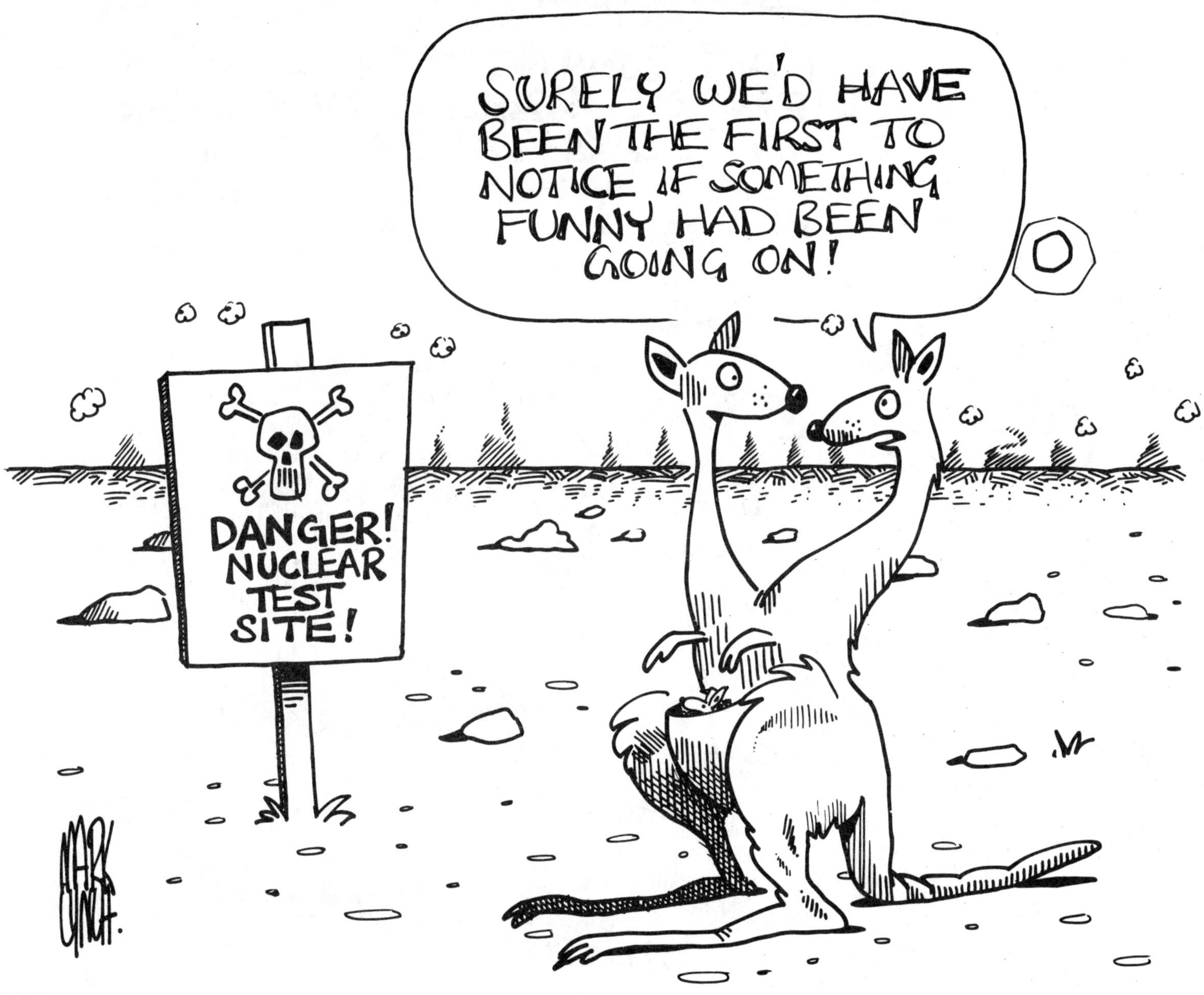
SURELY WE'D HAVE BEEN THE FIRST TO NOTICE IF SOMETHING FUNNY HAD BEEN GOING ON!
DANGER! NUCLEAR TEST SITE!

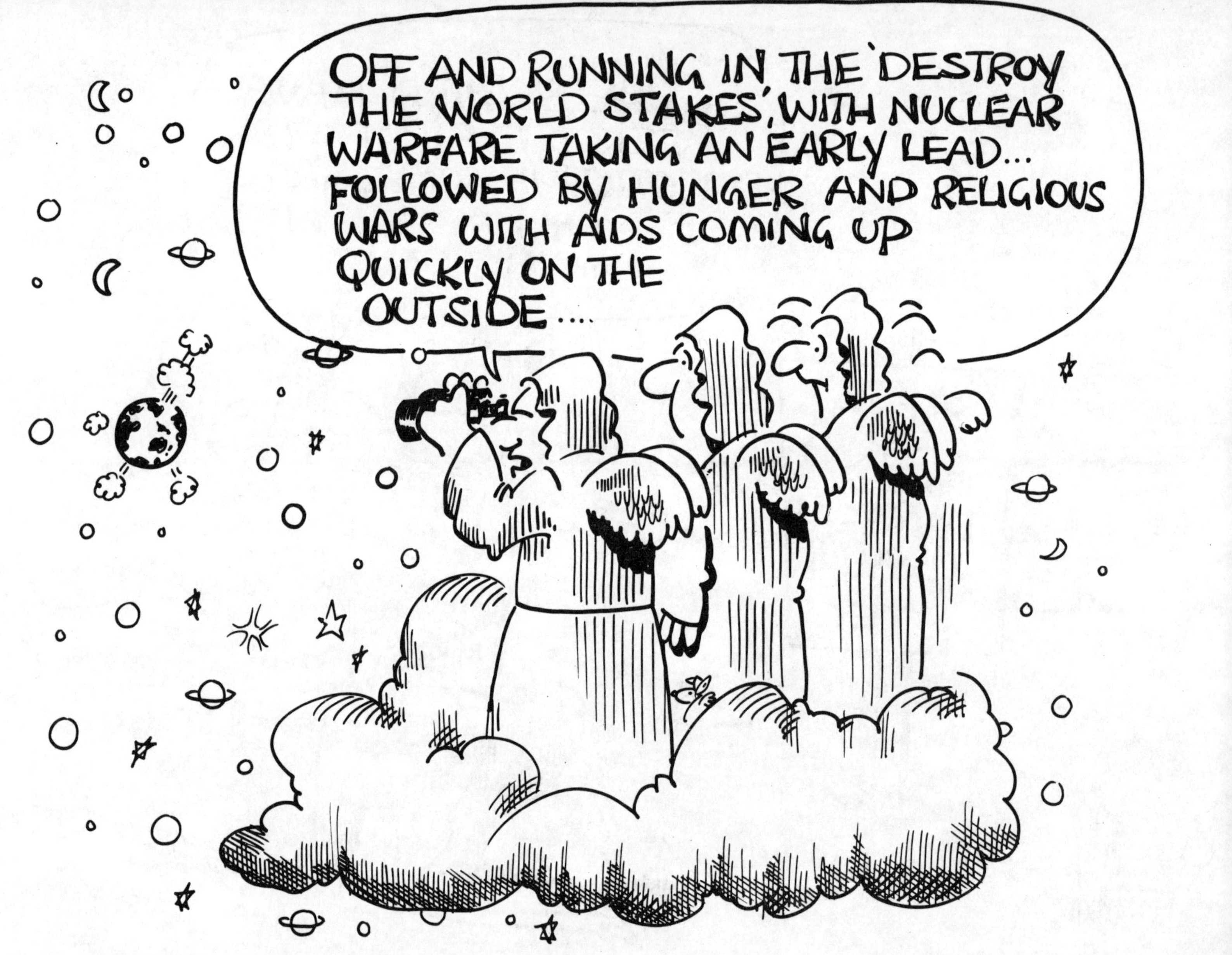
OFF AND RUNNING IN THE 'DESTROY THE WORLD STAKES', WITH NUCLEAR WARFARE TAKING AN EARLY LEAD... FOLLOWED BY HUNGER AND RELIGIOUS WARS WITH AIDS COMING UP QUICKLY ON THE OUTSIDE....

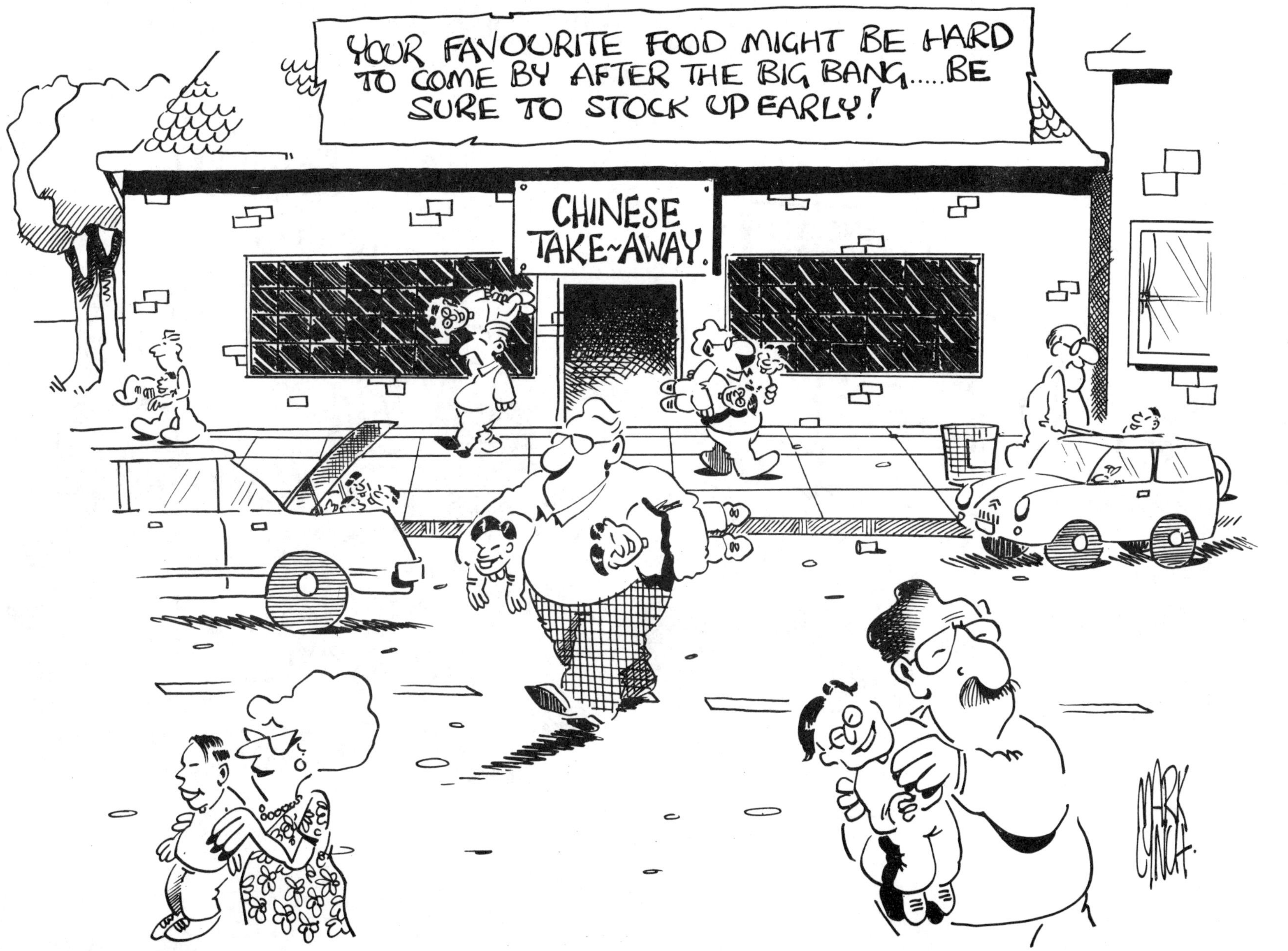
YOUR FAVOURITE FOOD MIGHT BE HARD TO COME BY AFTER THE BIG BANG.....BE SURE TO STOCK UP EARLY!
CHINESE TAKE~AWAY
MARK LYNCH

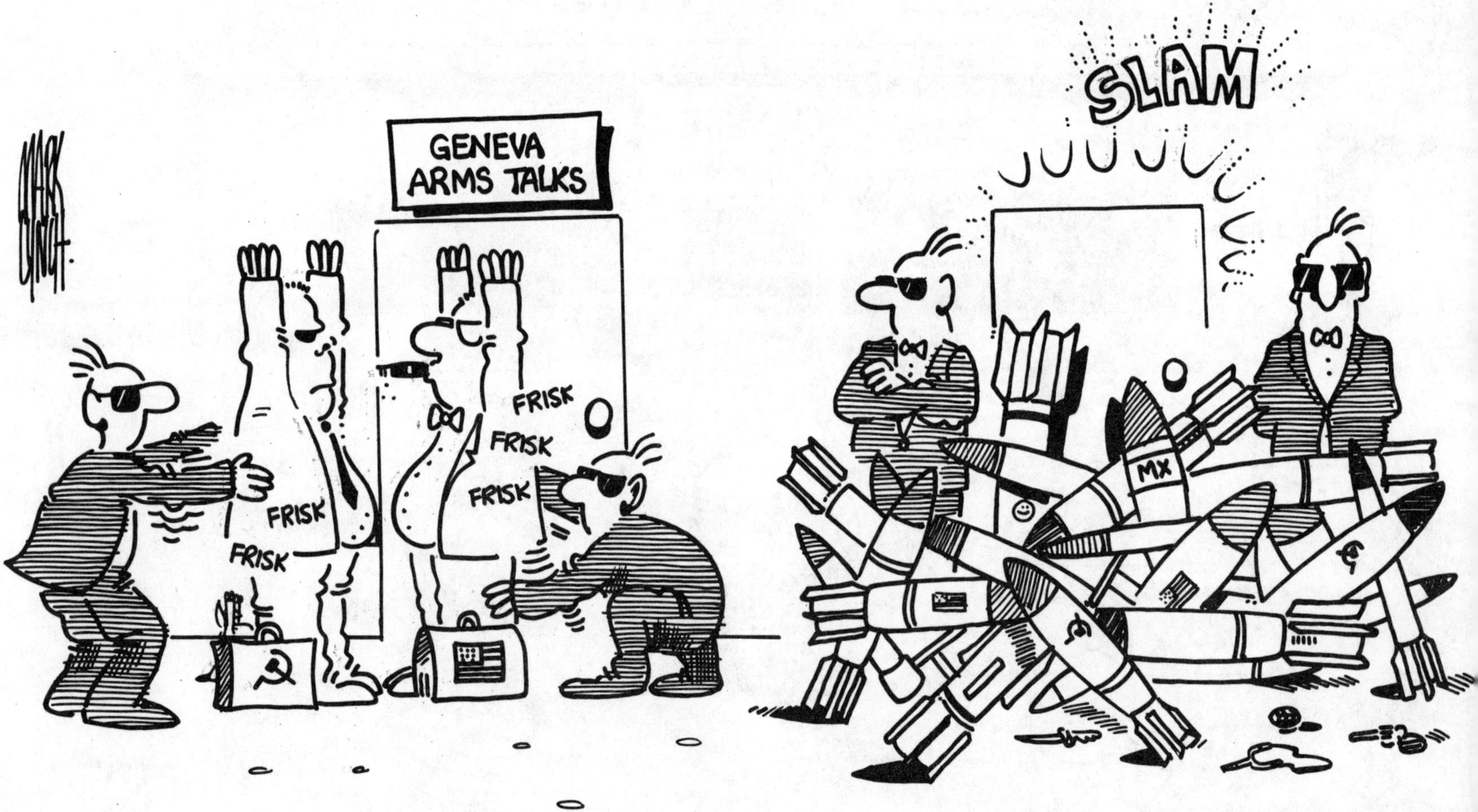
GENEVA
ARMS TALKS
FRISK
FRISK
FRISK
FRISK
FRISK
SLAM
MX

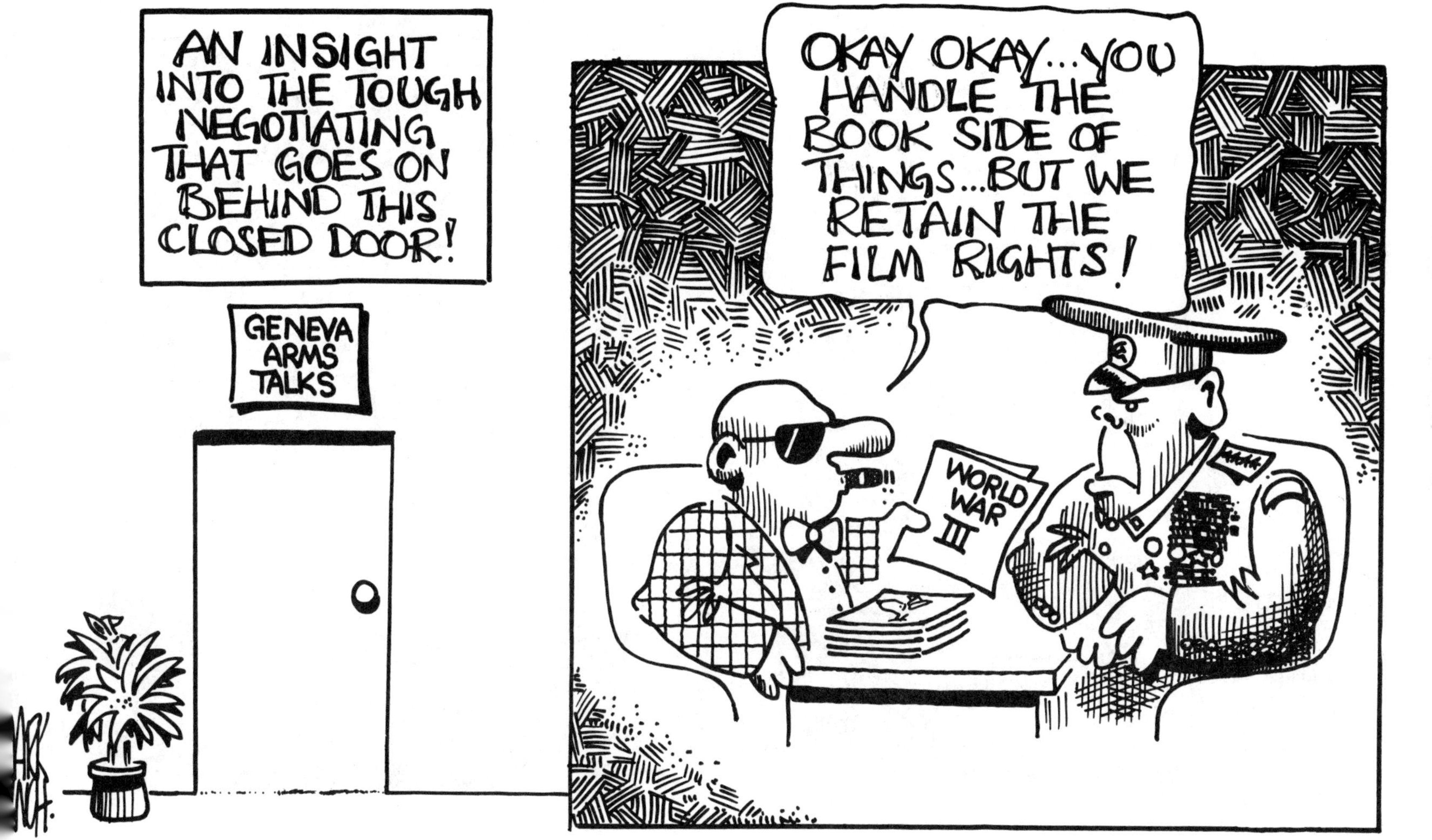
AN INSIGHT INTO THE TOUGH NEGOTIATING THAT GOES ON BEHIND THIS CLOSED DOOR!
GENEVA ARMS TALKS
OKAY OKAY...YOU HANDLE THE BOOK SIDE OF THINGS...BUT WE RETAIN THE FILM RIGHTS!
WORLD WAR III

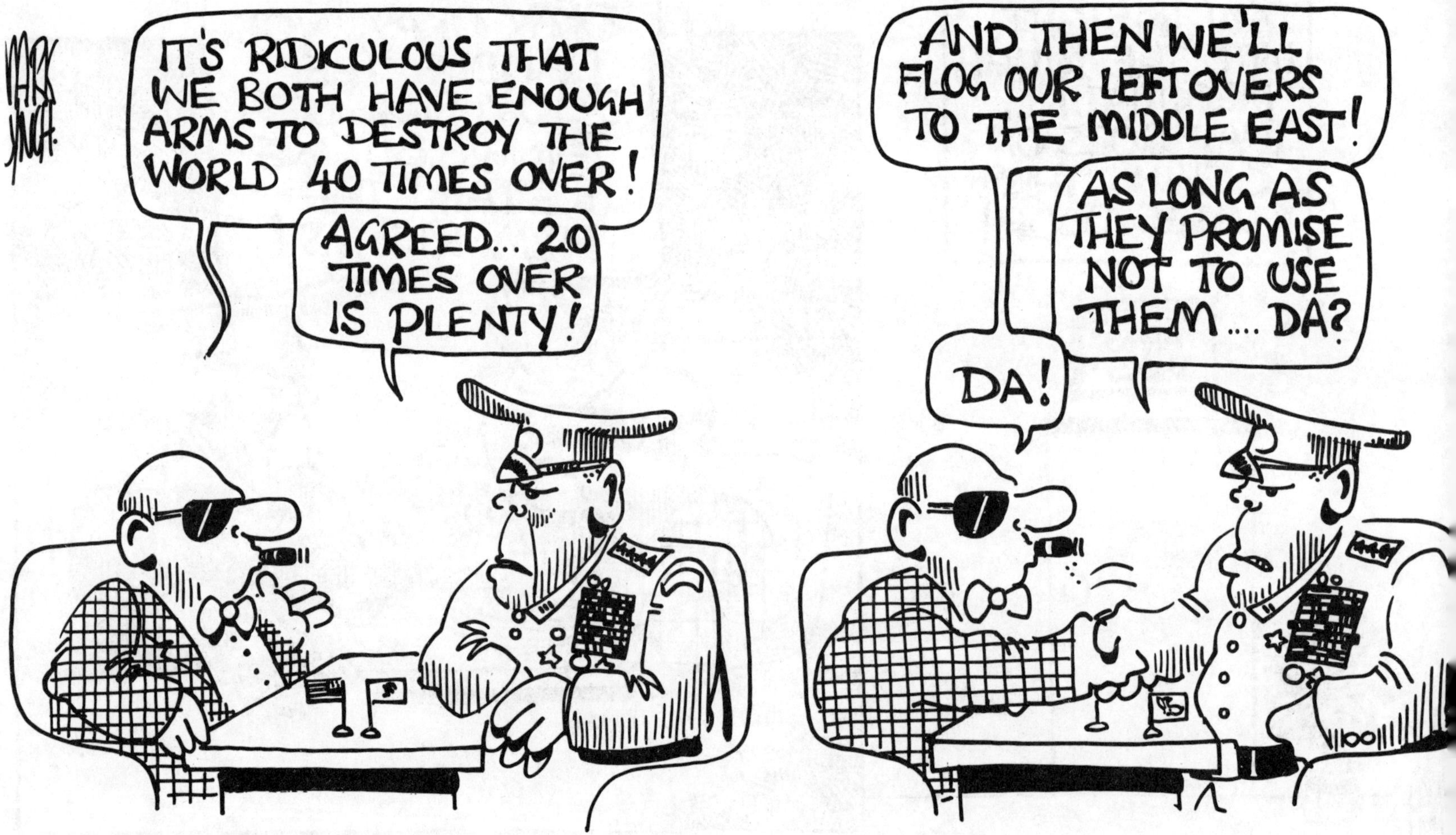
IT'S RIDICULOUS THAT WE BOTH HAVE ENOUGH ARMS TO DESTROY THE WORLD 40 TIMES OVER!
AGREED... 20 TIMES OVER IS PLENTY!
AND THEN WE'LL FLOG OUR LEFTOVERS TO THE MIDDLE EAST!
AS LONG AS THEY PROMISE NOT TO USE THEM.... DA?
DA!

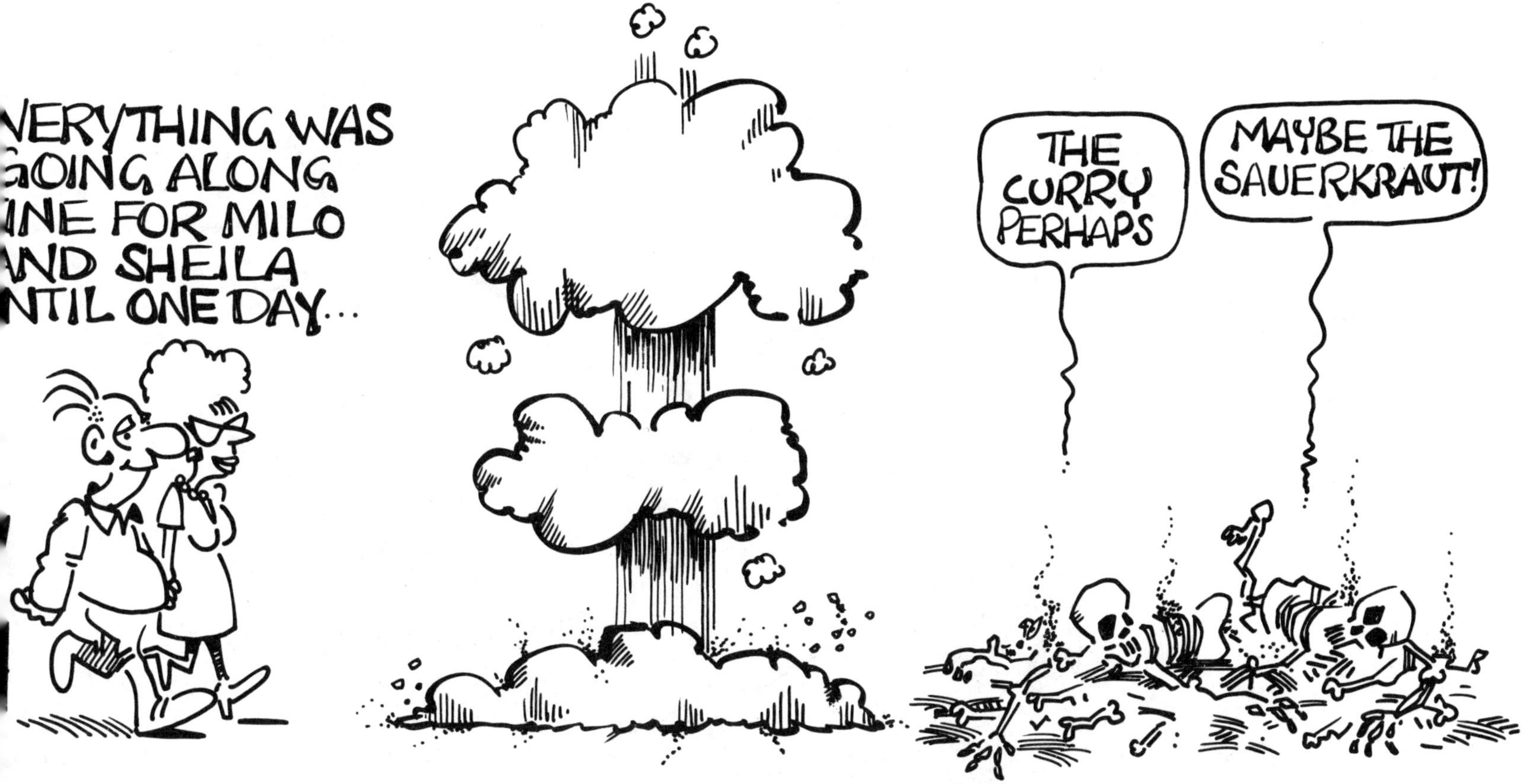
VERYTHING WAS GOING ALONG INE FOR MILO AND SHEILA NTIL ONE DAY...
THE CURRY PERHAPS
MAYBE THE SAUERKRAUT!

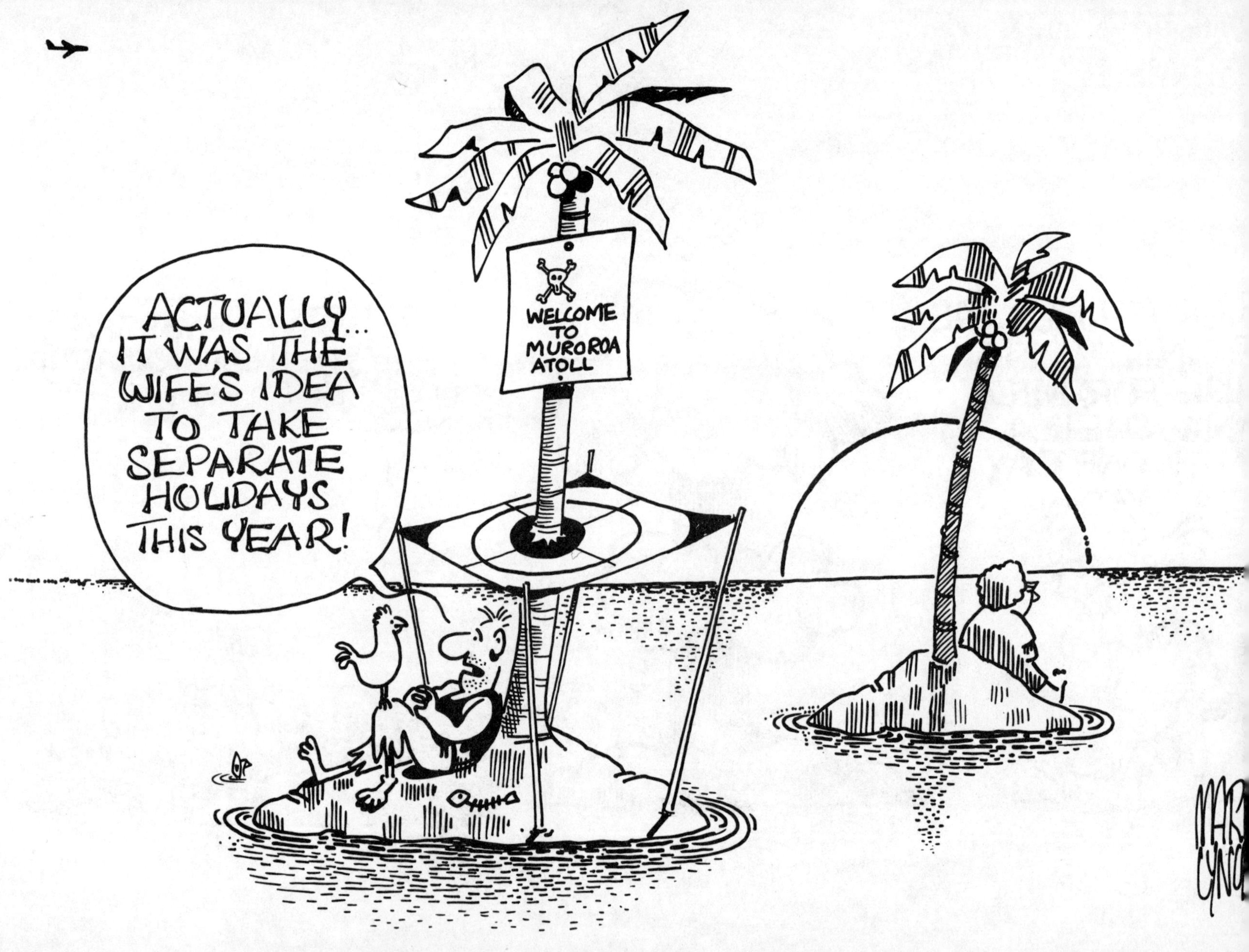
WELCOME TO MUROROA ATOLL
ACTUALLY... IT WAS THE WIFE'S IDEA TO TAKE SEPARATE HOLIDAYS THIS YEAR!

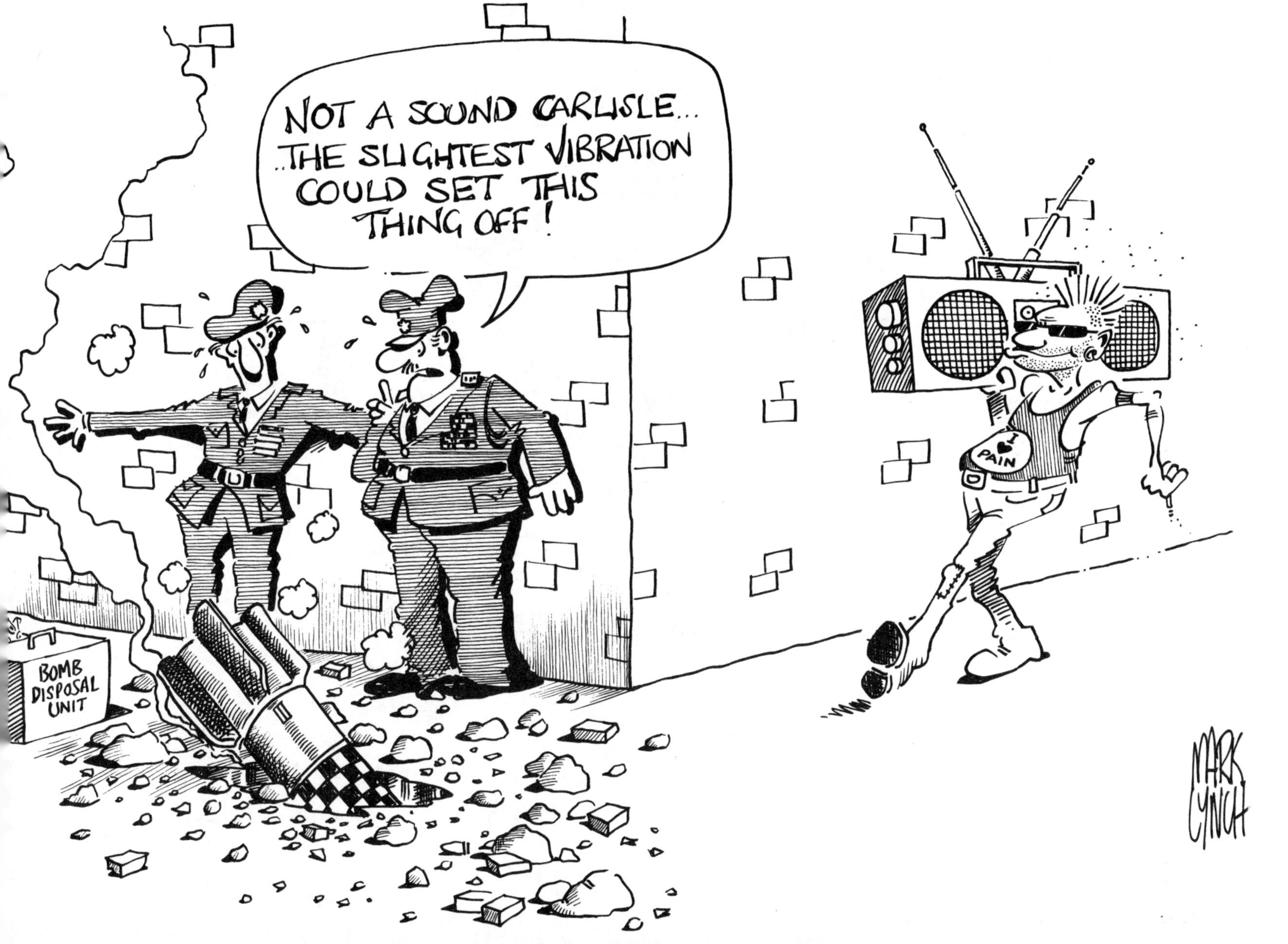
NOT A SOUND CARLISLE... ..THE SLIGHTEST VIBRATION COULD SET THIS THING OFF!
BOMB DISPOSAL UNIT
I ♥ PAIN
MARK LYNCH

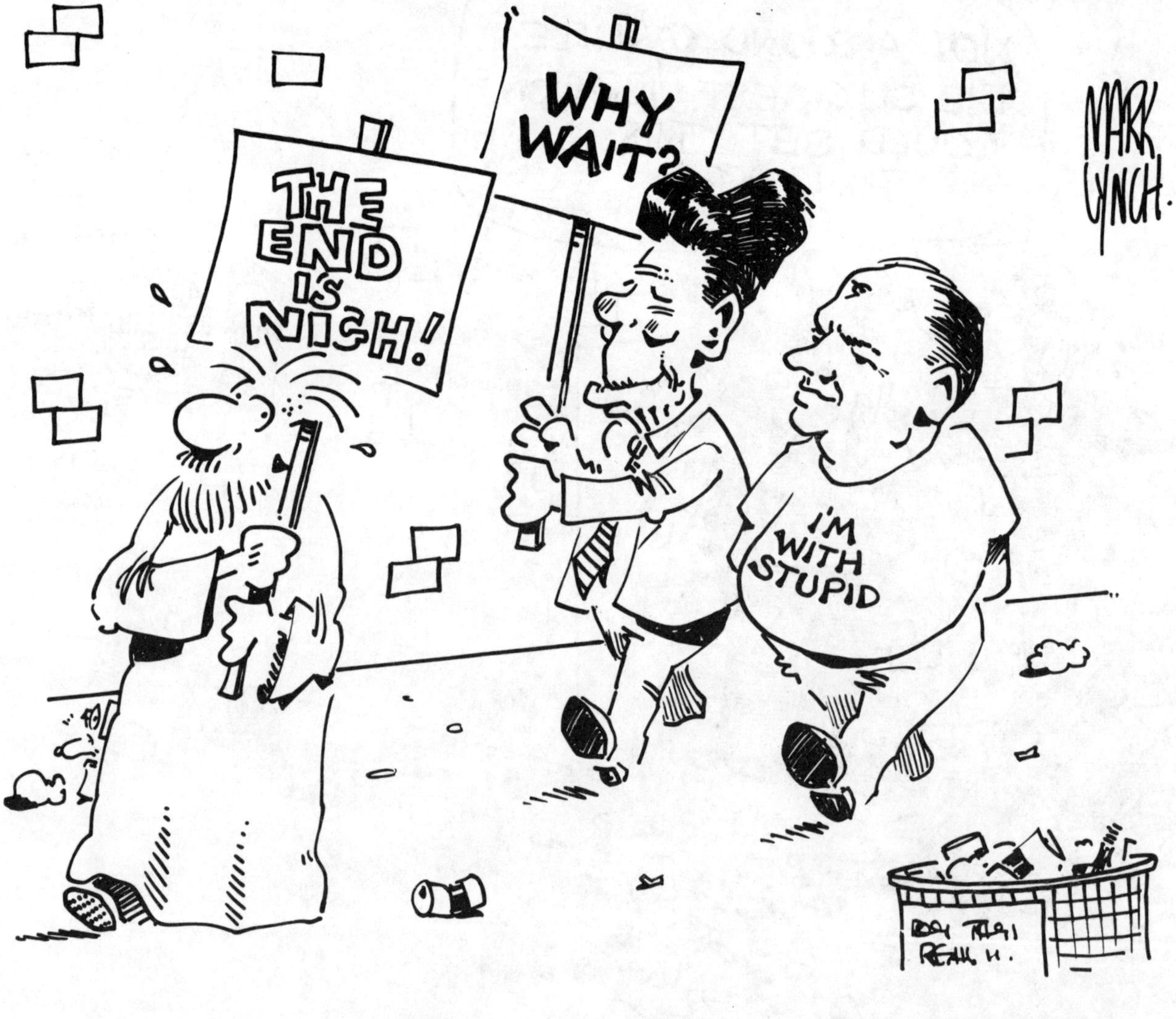
THE END IS NIGH!
WHY WAIT?
I'M WITH STUPID
MARK LYNCH.

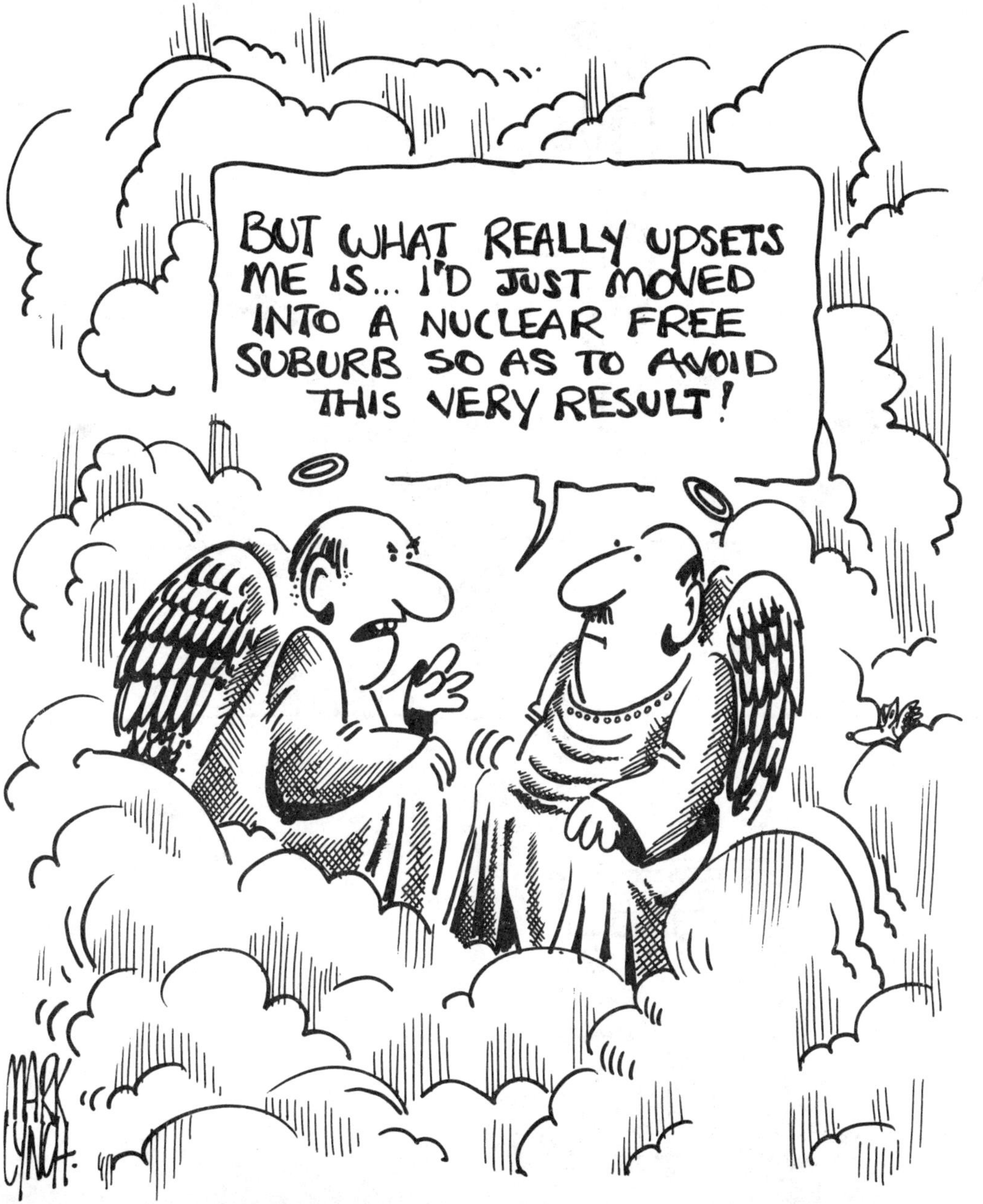
BUT WHAT REALLY UPSETS ME IS... I'D JUST MOVED INTO A NUCLEAR FREE SUBURB SO AS TO AVOID THIS VERY RESULT!
MARK LYNCH.

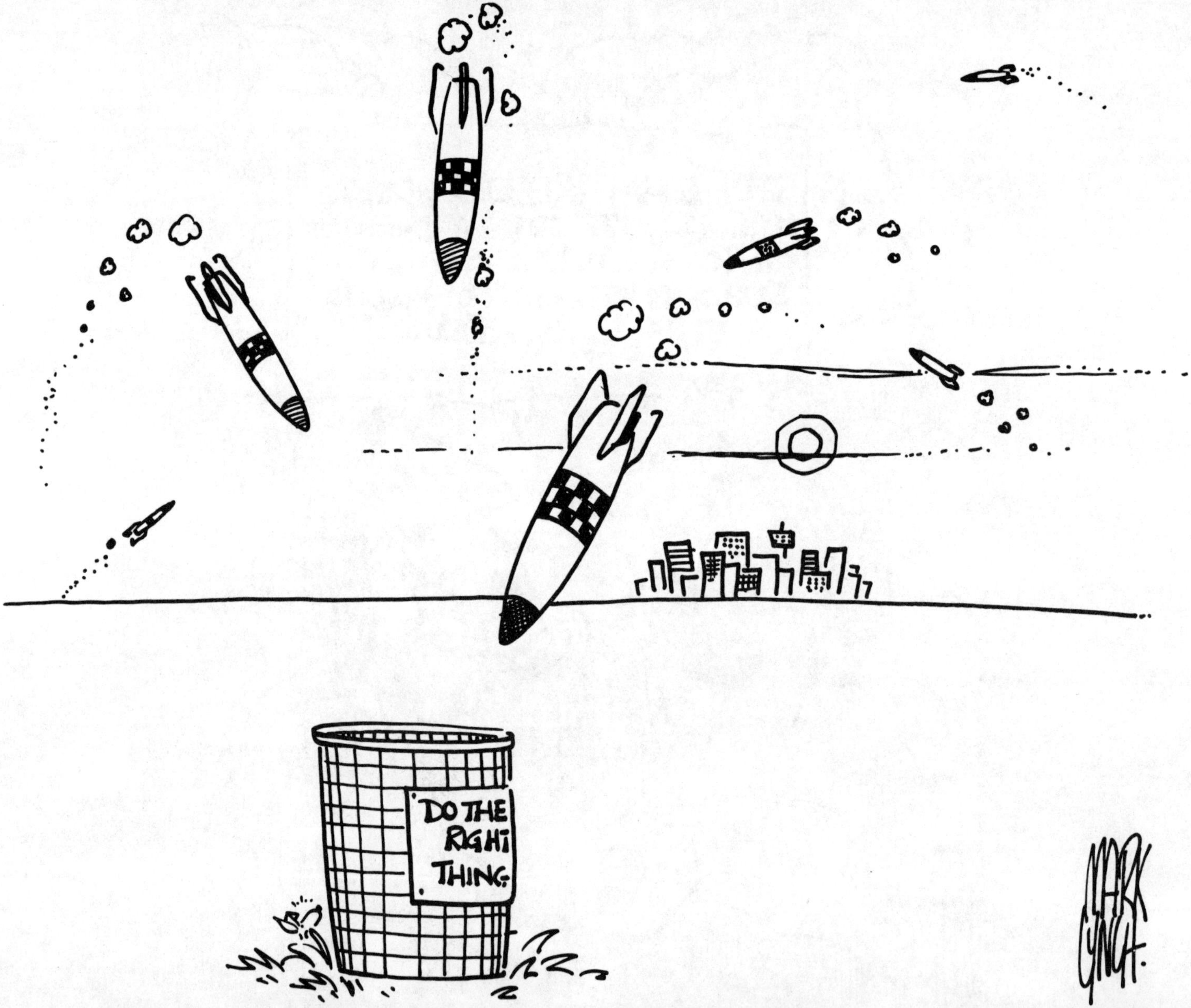
DO THE RIGHT THING.
MARK LYNCH.

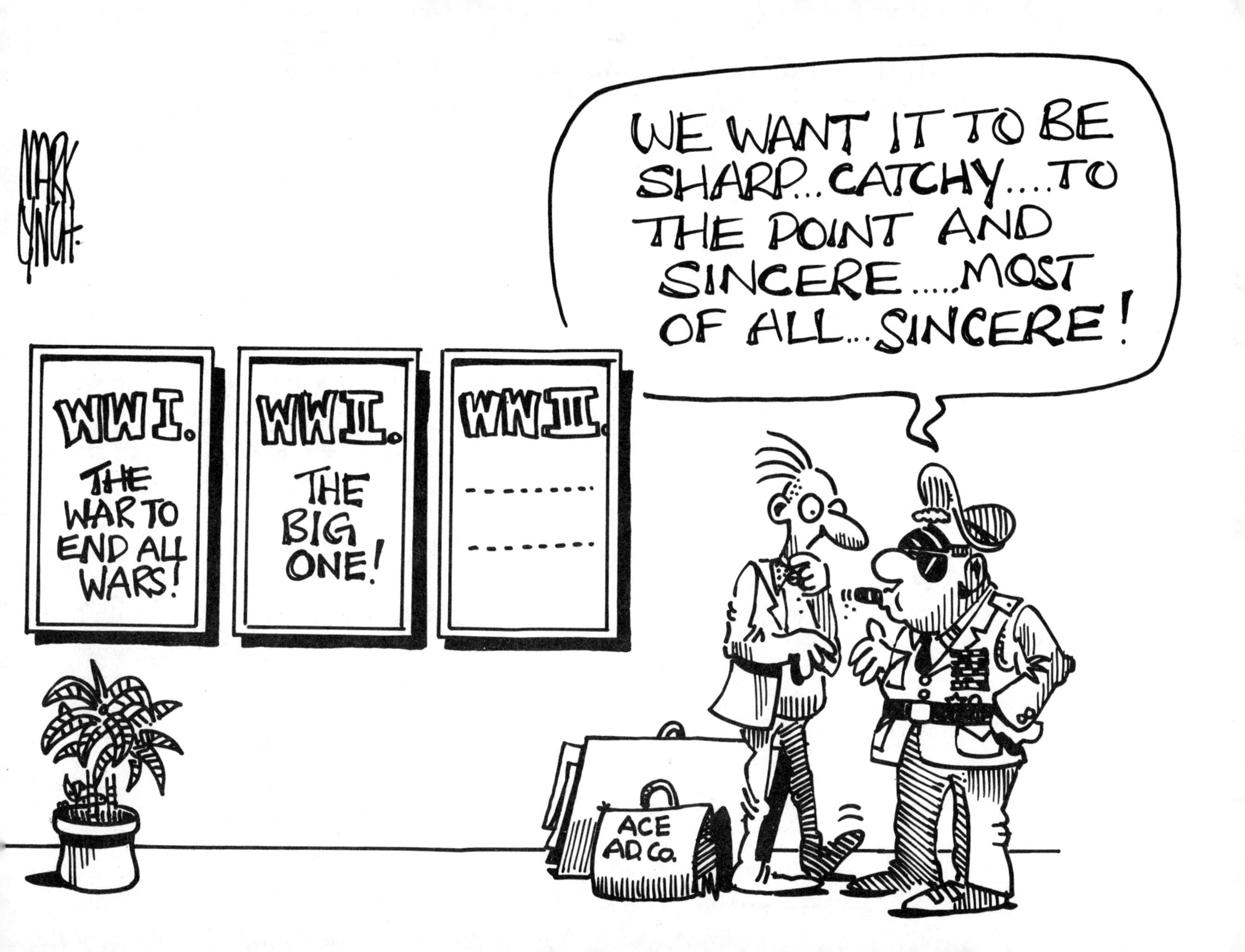
MARK LYNCH.
WE WANT IT TO BE SHARP... CATCHY..... TO THE POINT AND SINCERE..... MOST OF ALL... SINCERE!
WW I. THE WAR TO END ALL WARS!
WW II. THE BIG ONE!
WW III.
ACE AD Co.

AND THEN CAME CHERNOBYL!

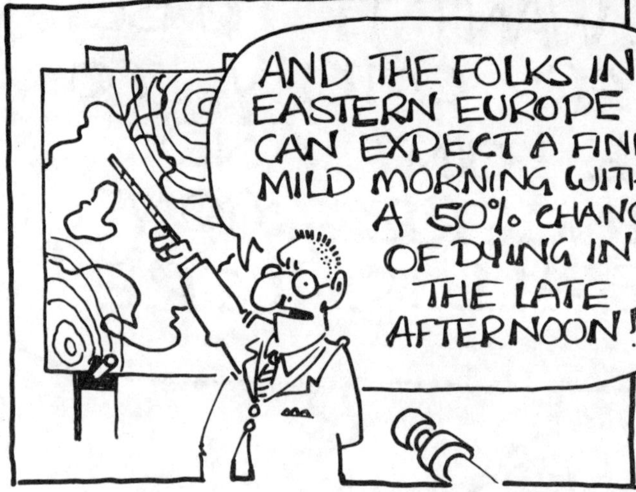
AND THE FOLKS IN EASTERN EUROPE CAN EXPECT A FINE, MILD MORNING WITH A 50% CHANCE OF DYING IN THE LATE AFTERNOON!

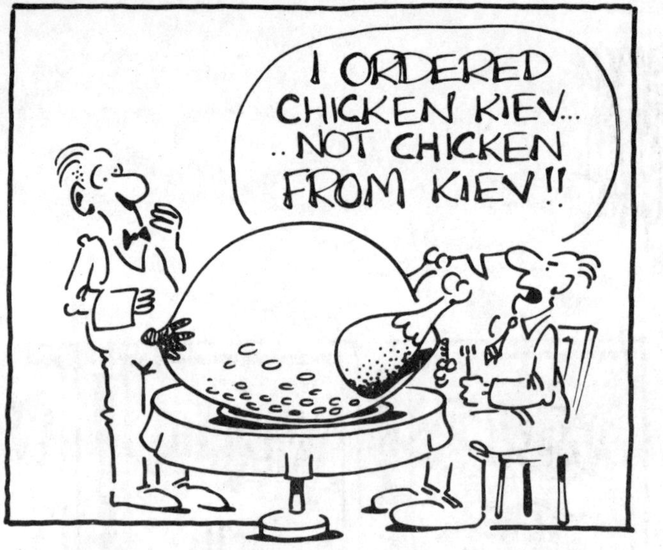
I ORDERED CHICKEN KIEV... ...NOT CHICKEN FROM KIEV!!

I AM worried about radioactive fall-out from this burnt out Soviet atomic power station. Should my family move to one of the socialist-controlled boroughs where the council says this sort of thing cannot happen because they have designated their zone nuclear free?

R. Samuels

(letter, *London Standard*)

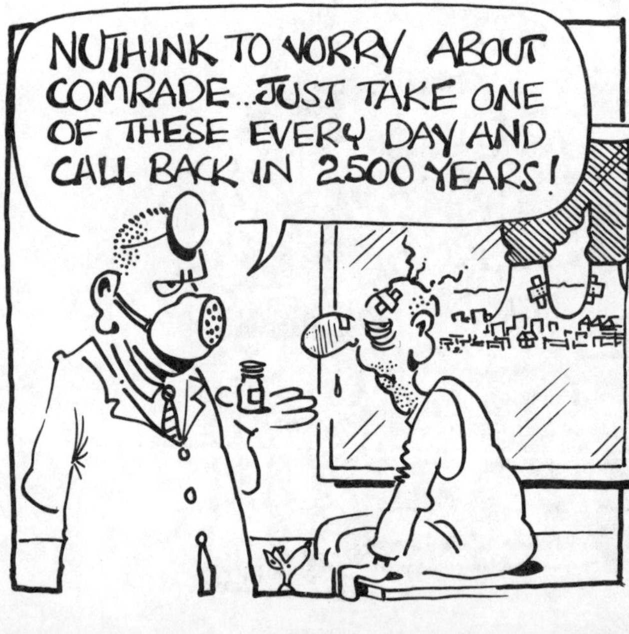
NUTHINK TO VORRY ABOUT COMRADE...JUST TAKE ONE OF THESE EVERY DAY AND CALL BACK IN 2500 YEARS!

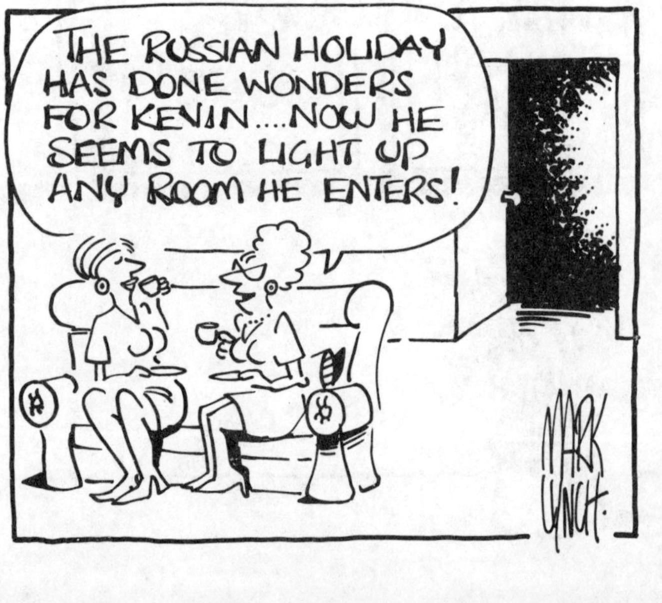
THE RUSSIAN HOLIDAY HAS DONE WONDERS FOR KEVIN....NOW HE SEEMS TO LIGHT UP ANY ROOM HE ENTERS!
MARK LYNCH.

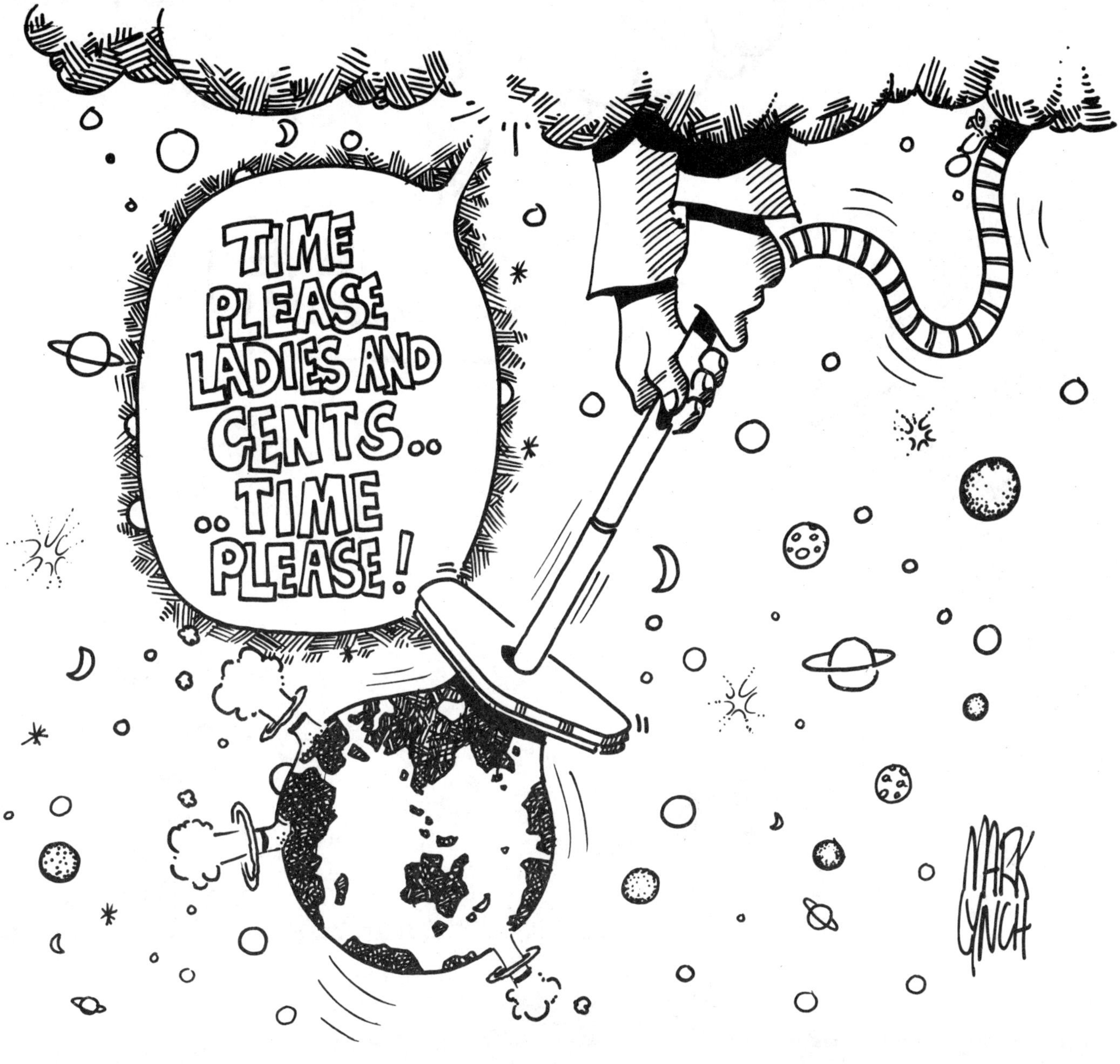
TIME PLEASE LADIES AND CENTS.. ..TIME PLEASE!
MARK LYNCH

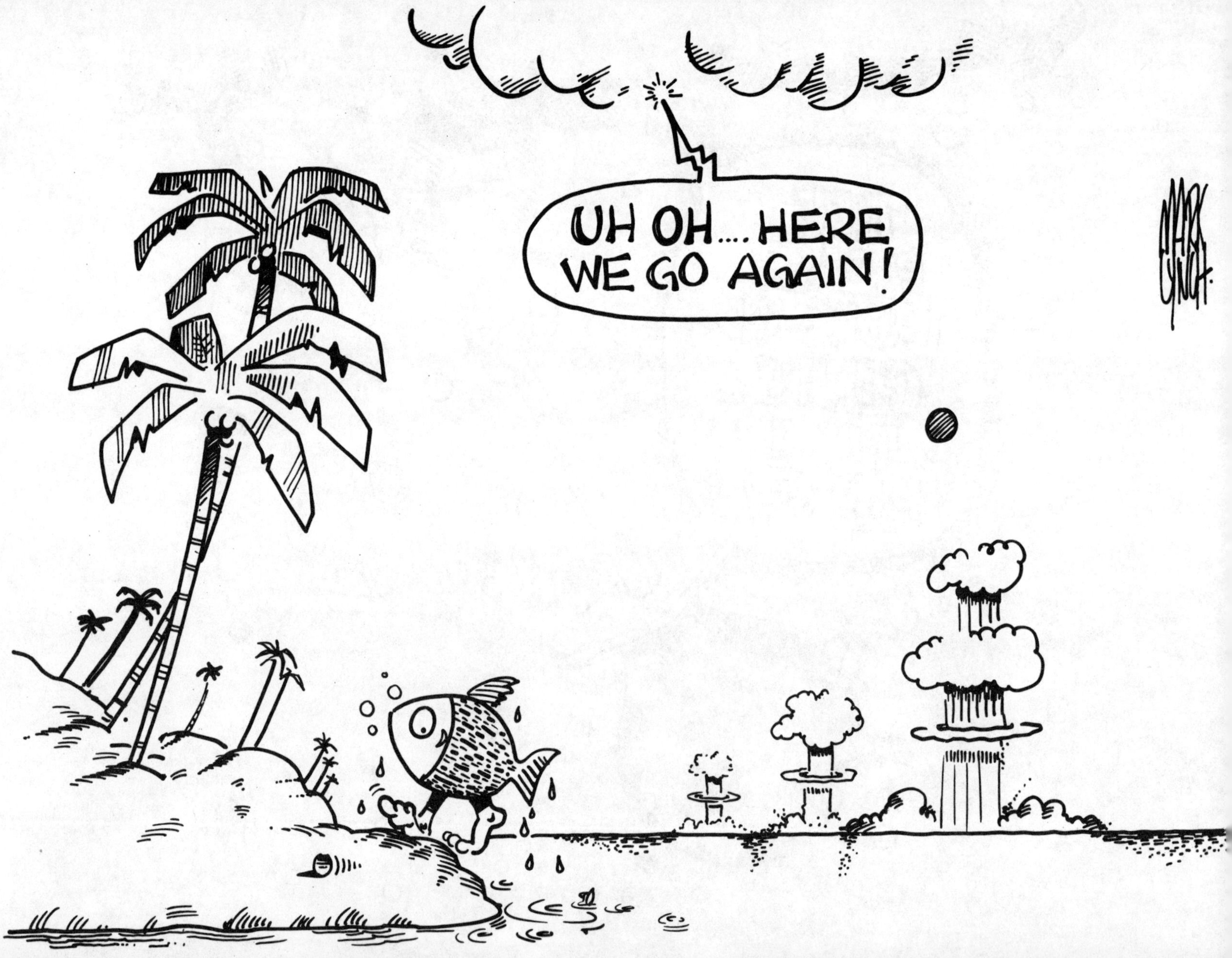
UH OH.... HERE WE GO AGAIN!